# BEAVER RIVER COUNTRY

# BEAVER RIVER
# COUNTRY

## An Adirondack History

## Edward I. Pitts

Syracuse University Press

∞ The paper used in this publication meets the minimum requirements
of the American National Standard for Information Sciences—Permanence
of Paper for Printed Library Materials, ANSI Z39.48-1992.

For a listing of books published and distributed by Syracuse University Press,
visit https://press.syr.edu/.

ISBN: 978-0-8156-3718-9 (hardcover)
978-0-8156-1133-2 (paperback)
978-0-8156-5537-4 (e-book)

**Library of Congress Cataloging-in-Publication Data**

Names: Pitts, Edward I., author.
Title: The Beaver River country : an Adirondack history / Edward I. Pitts.
Description: First edition. | Syracuse, New York : Syracuse University Press, [2022] |
Includes bibliographical references and index. | Summary: "This book is the first comprehensive
history of the remote section of the western Adirondacks surrounding the upper reaches
of the Beaver River. It contains the previously untold stories of early settlement, the advent
of sporting tourism, the creation of the Stillwater Reservoir, the effects of the coming
of the railroad, the vanished Beaver River Club, the Rap-Shaw Club and much more,
all illustrated with rare vintage photographs"— Provided by publisher.
Identifiers: LCCN 2021062659 (print) | LCCN 2021062660 (ebook) |
ISBN 9780815611332 (paperback) | ISBN 9780815637189 (hardcover) |
ISBN 9780815655374 (ebook)
Subjects: LCSH: Beaver River Region (N.Y.)—History. | Adirondack Mountains Region (N.Y.)—
History. | Tourism—New York (State)—Adirondack Mountains Region—History.
Classification: LCC F127.A2 P58 2022  (print) | LCC F127.A2  (ebook) |
DDC 974.7/5—dc23/eng/20220204
LC record available at https://lccn.loc.gov/2021062659
LC ebook record available at https://lccn.loc.gov/2021062660

*Manufactured in the United States of America*

# Contents

# Illustrations

# Acknowledgments

This book would not exist were it not for the steadfast encouragement of my wife Meredith Leonard. She not only provided moral support; she accompanied me on research trips and offered many helpful suggestions and editorial corrections.

During the research process I received assistance from many people who gave willingly of their time and expertise. The first person to materially assist me was Mary Kunsler-Larman of Canastota and Beaver River, New York. Mary freely shared her large collection of maps, photographs, and other memorabilia, and reviewed early drafts of several chapters.

In the hamlet of Stillwater I was assisted by retired DEC Ranger Terry Perkins, who lent his extensive knowledge of the woods and his stories and memories of the characters who are the soul of the Beaver River country. Other Stillwater and Beaver River residents who assisted me by providing information, criticism, and suggestions include Jim and Carol Fox, Dennis Buckley, Scott Thompson, Virginia Thompson, Marian Romano, Nate Vary, Jeff Fox, and Frank Rudolph. Crista Caldwell, summer resident of Beaver Lake, provided information and a private cottage tour to familiarize me with that area.

I also owe a debt of gratitude to the many local historians who assisted me in my search for old records, newspaper clippings, postcards, deeds, and other documents. Special thanks are due to Kate Lewis, director of the Town of Webb Historical Association, and assistant director Kristy Rubyor, who went above and beyond in combing their collection and making helpful comments. Local historians Charlie Herr of Inlet and Noel Sherry of Twitchell Lake also made valuable suggestions. The staff of the county clerk's offices in Herkimer and Onondaga Counties were helpful and tolerant of my search for old deeds, maps, and other records.

A special thanks is due to the people who gave me access to their vintage photograph collections and permission to reproduce their rare images. Thank you, Jim and Carol Fox, Frank Carey, Dennis Buckley, Tim Mayers, Paul Nance of St. Paul's Church in Albany, and Michael Hess. I also had free access to the Rap-Shaw Club's large photography archive.

Finally, I'd like to thank Neal Burdick for carefully editing the manuscript. His extensive knowledge of Adirondack history and his editorial skill significantly helped to shape the book.

Thanks to you all.

# BEAVER RIVER COUNTRY

# Introduction

I first came to the Beaver River country somewhat by accident about fifteen years ago. My wife and I made one of those spur-of-the-moment decisions prompted by a dotted line on our gazetteer. The winding two-lane blacktop from Eagle Bay ended at Big Moose Station. We decided to take a chance on the gravel road that led farther into the forest. It was a slow, dusty drive to the parking lot at Stillwater Reservoir. Even though it was a Sunday in mid-summer, there were only a handful of cars in the lot, plus a few empty boat trailers.

We stood looking across a magnificent stretch of water flanked by nothing but unbroken forest. On the far eastern horizon we could just barely make out the High Peaks of the Adirondacks.

The sound of a motor caught our attention. In a moment a large homemade metal barge carrying three pickup trucks appeared from behind a group of islands. An improbably small motorboat pushed the barge ashore. A spry fellow lowered a rusted steel gangway onto the gravel so the trucks could be on their way.

"Where did you come from?" I called to him.

"Beaver River," was all he replied.

We've been back to the Beaver River country every summer since. We have even made a few winter trips. Fourteen years ago, my wife and I joined the Rap-Shaw Club, which has a traditional outdoors camp on two islands in the reservoir. On our first visits there we met members whose families had been coming to the club for generations. Over the next years I gradually got to know many of the folks who have businesses and camps at Stillwater or at Beaver River.

1

Every time we have visited, I have wondered how it was possible that a place containing so much untamed wilderness could still exist. Little by little I pieced together the story.

This book is the first comprehensive history of the upper Beaver River valley. It contains a wealth of information not readily available elsewhere. The stories of the people who visited and lived in the area over the past two hundred years form the deep fabric of today's Beaver River country. Until now these stories have been a missing piece of the larger Adirondack history.

As far as possible this book is based on primary sources. This was made possible in part by the recent growth of a substantial online archive of early newspapers, books, and magazines. Most early reports from state agencies are now readily accessible, as are the nineteenth-century Adirondack guidebooks. Detailed endnotes provide a guide to the sources I consulted, for those who wish to refer to these old texts themselves.

Important parts of the story of the Beaver River country have never before been written down. Fortunately, a number of longtime residents preserved these stories in memory and in family archives. Discovering these archives was an adventure in itself. Several keepers of these family archives graciously spent many hours with me answering questions. They also gave me permission to publish selected photographs from their private collections.

This book will be of the most interest to those already somewhat acquainted with Beaver River, Stillwater, and Number Four / Beaver Lake. Although the area is very sparsely populated, thousands of visitors come to enjoy the Beaver River wilderness during every season. Spring brings those in search of smallmouth bass and hardy campers looking for solitude. Summer brings boaters and family camping groups. Fall brings leaf peepers and a small band of hunters. Winter is the season of snowmobiles.

People who have never visited the Beaver River country will find this book interesting if they have even a passing interest in Adirondack history. Many of the themes discussed have a general application to the entire Adirondacks. For example, the chapter on the building of the Stillwater Reservoir forms a part of a larger story of wilderness preservation. The chapter on the Rap-Shaw Club echoes similar stories from outdoors clubs all across the Adirondacks, while the chapter on the Beaver River Club provides an in-depth view of an important social institution that flourished and then, like many, completely vanished.

Outdoors tourists have been coming to the Beaver River country for almost two hundred years. The first sporting tourists came primarily to hunt and fish. Women soon joined in the fun and in short order whole families were enjoying camping together. It didn't take long before outdoors tourism was the economic foundation of the area. Tourists hired guides and rented hotel rooms. Many of the visitors returned year after year. Some built simple camps, some a wilderness clubhouse, and some an elegant club and cottages.

At times the survival of the wilderness that attracted visitors has been challenged by the economic forces of the outside world. Lumbering came to the area beginning about 1850 but ended up being restricted to only part of the region. The waterpower needs of industries on the Black River led to the creation of a large reservoir that flooded one of the most picturesque areas of the river. The acquisition of large tracts of wilderness around the upper river threatened for a brief time to end outdoors tourism altogether.

The complex interplay of economics, outdoors tourism, and wilderness preservation pervade every section of this book. Fortunately, each successive generation of residents and visitors eventually discovered the central importance of preserving the river, the lakes, and the forest. To a surprising degree, some of the most pivotal decisions were the result of happenstance, not deliberate planning. In a time when the remaining Adirondack wilderness is increasingly imperiled, it is important to know how and why so much of the Beaver River wilderness survived.

This book is divided into five slightly overlapping but generally chronological parts. The chapters are arranged so that the book can be read as a whole and then be used as a reference.

The first part, "Wilderness," begins by describing the Beaver River country as it existed prior to European settlement. It discusses how glaciation created the physical features of the Beaver River valley, then reviews the area's long Native American occupation. It discusses in detail the important first land purchases and describes the earliest settlement of the pioneer village of Number Four. Finally, it tells the stories of the two hermits who lived along the wild upper Beaver River before 1860.

Beaver River tourism started with a trickle in the mid-1830s, became a steady flow by 1850, and turned into a flood in the 1870s and 1880s. The second part, "Early Tourists," provides the history of the oldest foot trail and the first roads. It describes the earliest influx of sporting tourists and gives examples from the first-person accounts of four important early visitors. This part concludes with a discussion of all of the Beaver River county's earliest sportsmen's hotels.

The third part, "Dams, Railroad, and Beaver River Station," begins by providing the first complete history of the series of dams that created the impoundment of the Beaver River at Stillwater. It then discusses the important role played by Dr. William Seward Webb and his railroad in bringing in a new generation of tourists. It concludes with a history of the founding and early days of the hamlet created by the railroad, Beaver River Station.

The fourth part, "Private Clubs," tells the stories of two unique outdoors clubs that attracted scores of members and guests to the Beaver River country. It begins by describing the exclusive Beaver River Club, which rose on the shores of the 1893–94 impoundment and was later destroyed when the reservoir was expanded. Indeed, few of the many Adirondack sportsmen's clubs founded in the later part of the nineteenth century survive today. The Rap-Shaw Club not only survived many adversities but actually flourished while making the transition from a male-only hunting and fishing club to the family outdoors club of today.

The fifth part, "Settlement at Stillwater," describes the evolution of the Stillwater Hotel from its first version in 1902 until the present. It explains the conditions that gave rise to the hamlet of Stillwater, discusses how the facilities there today came about, and concludes with a brief review of key features of the present hamlets of Stillwater and Beaver River.

The Beaver River country of the west-central Adirondacks is one of those rare places where the great northern wilderness survives nearly intact. There are large tracts of climax forest that never felt the blows of the lumberman's ax. Dozens of lakes repose nearly undisturbed by human visitation since the time of the glaciers. If you already know and love the Beaver River country, this book will provide you with a deeper perspective. If you are thinking of visiting for the first time, it will open your eyes to a different and wilder side of the Adirondacks.

# Part One

# Wilderness

1. On the Beaver River before the scenery was destroyed by the state dam, uncredited photograph. *Eighth and Ninth Reports of the Forest, Fish and Game Commission (1902–1903)* (Albany, NY: J. B. Lyon Company, Printers), facing p. 288.

# 1

# The Wild Beaver River Country

## The Beaver River Wilderness

This is the story of an improbable wilderness. The Beaver River country in the west-central Adirondacks of New York has survived as mostly wilderness from the end of the last ice age to the present. Massive glaciers carved the valley where the Beaver River now flows, and created the many natural lakes. Centuries ago, a great mixed northern forest colonized the rocky soil as the climate warmed. Whitetail deer, moose, elk, black bear, wolves, fishers, river otter, beaver, and many more northern species moved back north and flourished in great numbers. The cold free-flowing river and nearby lakes became the home of millions of brook trout.

Human beings were attracted to this abundant forest. The ancestors of today's Haudenosaunee people came to hunt and fish thousands of years ago. Long before the arrival of Europeans, the Beaver River valley was the territory of the Indigenous Oneida and Mohawk peoples.[1] They often traveled the area, but little evidence remained of their passing save for a well-worn foot trail connecting to the next watershed to the north, the Oswegatchie. People of European ancestry did not begin to explore the area until the beginning of the nineteenth century.

In most of the northeastern United States, settlement by European peoples meant the end of the wilderness. In contrast, much of the wilderness survived along upper Beaver River as people came to love and protect it. Because of their efforts, the Beaver River country remains the wild beating heart of the Adirondacks.

9

To say that the Beaver River country is still mostly wilderness requires a bit of qualification.[2] From the last half of the nineteenth century up until the present, some of the land around the upper Beaver River has been logged. Early logging was initially confined to near the river. After the arrival of the railroad in 1892, logging became more widespread, but for reasons connected to the damming of the river to create a reservoir, a large part of the Beaver River valley escaped logging entirely.

The Beaver River country also has a long history of outdoors tourism, beginning in the early decades of the nineteenth century. Between 1892 and 1925 the territory became an especially popular destination for fishing and hunting. This activity also disturbed and transformed the original landscape.

Because of its history of resource extraction in the form of hunting, fishing, and logging, it is perhaps more accurate to call the Beaver River country a recovered wilderness. In accordance with the definitions adopted by the Adirondack Park Agency in its State Land Use Master Plan, almost all of the north side of the upper Beaver River is now classified as wilderness while most of the south side is classified as wild forest.[3]

## The Original Course of the River

The wild Beaver River can be geographically divided into three sections based on river topography. The headwaters section began with the streams flowing into Smith's Lake (now Lake Lila).[4] The Beaver River originally flowed freely out of Smith's Lake over a course of rapids before entering the wider end of Albany (now Nehasane) Lake. At the downstream outlet of Albany Lake, the river again became a stretch of shallow rapids called, then as now, Little Rapids. For most of the year these two sets of rapids were not navigable by canoe or guideboat, so they were bypassed on well-established carry trails.

The next section of the river was originally a flat marshland that began just below Little Rapids and stretched for about eleven miles to the west. This meandering section of the river was generally navigable

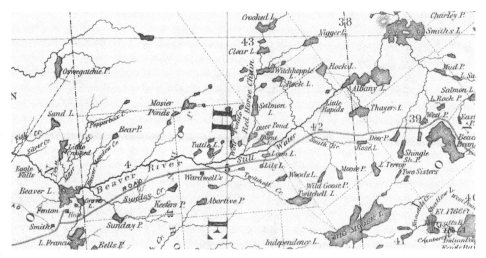

2. Detail from *Map of the New York Wilderness* by W. W. Ely showing the upper Beaver River before the dams. Wallace, *Guide* (New York: G. W. and C. B. Colton & Co., 1876).

but consisted of endless oxbows and beaver dams. It was said that it took twenty-two miles of paddling to accomplish eleven miles of forward progress.

About two miles downstream from Little Rapids, the South Branch of the Beaver River flowed into the main branch. About three miles farther downstream, the Red Horse Creek entered from the north. Throughout this section a large number of glacial eskers, moraines, and kames caused the river to meander right and then left to find the way downstream.[5]

The last mile or two at the west end of the great marsh between the confluence of Twitchell Creek and the downstream rapids was originally called the "still water" of the Beaver River, or the "Stillwater level." Verplanck Colvin, the pioneering Adirondack surveyor, had one of his survey parties prepare a map of the upper Beaver River in 1878.[6] As can be seen in the detail shown here, the still water included two substantial kettle hole ponds, Tuttle Pond on the north and a deep pond nearly bisected by a long esker on the south that Colvin named Stillwater Pond. A high bank rose to the east of this

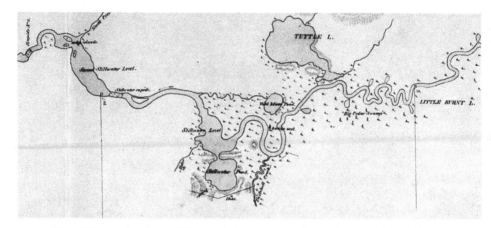

3. The Stillwater level, detail from 1878 survey map drawn by Frank Tweedy, CE, New York State Archives, Dept. of Environmental Conservation, Verplanck Colvin maps of the Adirondack wilderness, B1405-96, SARA No. 275, 276.

pond, separating it from the spot where Twitchell Creek meandered in from the south.

The narrow spit of higher ground shown on Colvin's map between Stillwater Pond and the confluence of Twitchell Creek and the Beaver River eventually would become the location of the first buildings in the Beaver River country east of the hamlet of Number Four. The location was picturesque. To the east, the marshy Beaver River stretched for miles, surrounded by low hills. In the far distance were the High Peaks. The open marsh was excellent deer habitat, and the meandering, clear river was home to thousands of brook trout. The entire area was surrounded by tens of thousands of acres of unbroken virgin northern forest.

At the west end of the Stillwater level, the river narrowed and then began a steep ten-mile descent. In this rugged third section, nineteen sets of steep rocky rapids and falls effectively prevented practical further downstream navigation to Beaver Lake. The tiny pioneer settlement of Number Four, founded in 1822, was at the west end of Beaver Lake.

Downstream from Beaver Lake the forest became less wild. Nearer the Black River, deep soil made farming feasible. As settlers moved into the Black River valley, the forest was cleared for pioneer farms. Upstream from Beaver Lake, the wild forest reigned supreme.

## Rocks and Glaciers

The Adirondacks are rocky. The metamorphic bedrock is Precambrian in origin, part of the Canadian Shield, formed fifteen miles deep in the earth 1.1 billion years ago.[7] It may be the oldest rock exposed on the surface of the earth.

Unlike elongated mountain ranges such as the Appalachians, the Adirondack range is a roughly circular, recently uplifted, dome about 160 miles wide. It is still moving upward at the rate of about three millimeters per year. That is pretty fast in geological terms and exceeds the average rate of erosion.

While the dome accounts for the overall oval shape of the Adirondack region, glaciers were primarily responsible for the specific surface features we see today. The glacial ice sheet gradually advanced southward through the Adirondack region, scraping soil and rock from the land and embedding it in the ice like sand in sandpaper. Alternately scarring and smoothing the earth's surface, the glacier raked giant pieces of rock from mountainsides, rounding them into boulders and pulverizing the rubble into pebbles and sand.

Then, about 12,000 years ago, the glaciers started to retreat. As the glaciers melted, the massive release of water cut the lakes and river valleys we know today. By about 11,000 years ago the ice had left the upper Beaver River valley. Between 10,200 and 9,600 years ago the northern forest redeveloped.[8]

As the great ice sheet melted and receded, it dropped the sand and smoothed rock it carried. Everywhere, large boulders, carried down from the north, littered the landscape, even on the tops of the highest mountains. These rocks, called glacial erratics, were deposited throughout the Adirondacks, where they can be seen today in fields, along forest trails, and scattered on mountainsides.

Nowhere in the Adirondacks are these features more pronounced than in the Beaver River country. The general location and course of the Beaver River is the direct result of the melting glacier. The islands and treacherous shoals of today's Stillwater Reservoir are the remains of the glacial deposits left behind as the last great glacier melted.

### Native Americans

As soon as the glaciers melted, life began to return to the scoured land. Plants and animals driven south thousands of years earlier slowly migrated north again. After a thousand years, meadows, wetlands, and forests once again covered the land. The glacier had carved hundreds of new lakes and ponds, many of which formed long navigable chains. New rivers and streams ran outward from the Adirondack dome in every direction.[9]

Human beings began to explore this reborn land as soon as wildlife returned. Little is known about these early people, but when the earliest Europeans arrived along the edges of the Adirondacks, they encountered Haudenosaunee people everywhere.[10] On the north, south, and east were the Mohawks. To the west along Lake Ontario and the Tug Hill plateau (to this day called the Lesser Wilderness) were the Onondagas. The west-central Adirondacks were the territory of the Oneidas. The Beaver River runs through the territories of both the Oneidas and the Mohawks; while Oneida territory included the Black River and part of the Beaver River, Mohawk territory included the upper Beaver River.

Perhaps because there were no existing Native American villages when white pioneers began to explore and map the Adirondacks, early Adirondack historians generally concluded that Native Americans built no settlements in the region. Donaldson's short chapter on the subject in *A History of the Adirondacks* claimed, based on dubious anecdotal evidence, there might have been only one temporary Indian settlement anywhere in the Adirondacks.[11] In *The Story of a Wilderness*, Grady noted there was abundant evidence that Iroquois frequented the Moose River Valley but nonetheless asserted that it was improbable that any Indian settlements ever existed in the central Adirondacks.[12] Sylvester carefully reviewed the earliest accounts of European contact

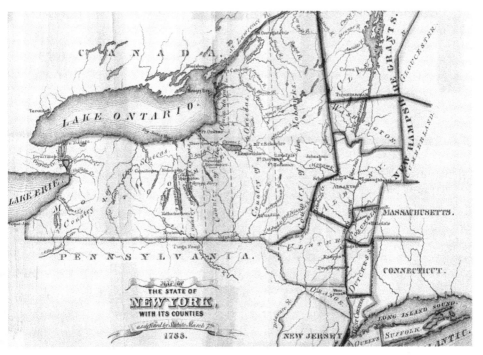

4. Map of the state of New York with its counties as defined by statute, March 7, 1788, printed by Hoffman & Knickerbocker, Albany, NY. New York State Archives, Series A0448-79, Recorded Indian treaties and deeds, 1703–1871 (bulk 1748–1871). Vol. 1, p. 1.

with Native Americans before he too concluded there was no evidence for the existence of Native American settlements anywhere in the region.[13] All three of these historians agreed, however, that up until the time of the American Revolution the Haudenosaunee extensively used the Adirondacks both as a hunting ground and as a passageway between Central New York and the St. Lawrence River Valley.

The majority view that there was no Haudenosaunee settlement in the Adirondacks is not without its critics. Inside the Six Nations Iroquois Cultural Center in Onchiota, New York, there sits the remains of an ancient dugout canoe recovered from a nearby lake bottom. If a visitor expresses interest in this artifact, one of the members of the Fadden family, owners of the museum, will be happy to explain their view.

"We have always been here," claims David Kanietakeron Fadden. He agrees that the Adirondacks were a passageway and hunting ground for his Mohawk ancestors, but he reasons that not everyone left when the weather turned cold in the fall. "They had food and water. They had shelter. For some people there was no reason to leave. Just like today, when the tourists leave, the natives settle in for the winter."[14]

The Faddens are not alone in their belief that Native Americans probably had a permanent presence in the Adirondacks long before white settlement. Scattered here and there in museums throughout New York are collections of Stone Age tools gathered from various Adirondack locations. A 1985 survey commissioned by the New York State Office of Parks, Recreation, and Historic Sites listed more than 350 probable early Native American habitation sites within the Adirondacks. Professional archaeologists have investigated only a small number of these sites.[15] It seems that the absence of an archaeological record of early Iroquoian Adirondack settlements is due in large part to inadequate research.

One person making a modest effort to remedy this deficit is Dr. Jay Curt Stager, a professor of biology at Paul Smith's College. Dr. Stager argues that a deeper, scientifically rigorous investigation of probable settlement locations is needed before conclusions can be drawn about Native American use of the Adirondacks.[16] To this end he and his students are engaged in preliminary investigations that are intended to uncover evidence of early human presence in the region.[17]

Whether or not there were Haudenosaunee settlements in the Adirondacks prior to European exploration and settlement, there are surprisingly few accounts of encounters between Europeans and either Mohawk or Oneida people in the great north woods. Following the American Revolution, just as Europeans were pushing into the region, the Haudenosaunee largely left the vast Adirondack territory they had claimed as their own for centuries. The reason was simple: New York State pushed them off the land through a series of questionable treaties.

The new federal government initially attempted to prevent New York from making land treaties with the Haudenosaunee residing within its borders. The Non-Intercourse Act of 1790 provided that the US federal government had the sole authority to regulate interactions between Native Americans and nonnatives. It prohibited the sale of Native American lands to individuals or states, absent formal federal approval. In the 1794 Treaty of Canandaigua, the federal government formally recognized the Haudenosaunee claim to as much as six million acres of their ancestral territory.

Federal law notwithstanding, New York continued treaty negotiations with the Haudenosaunee. In 1796, New York State signed a treaty with the Mohawks that extinguished that nation's remaining claim to virtually all of their territory in the Adirondacks. During the first two decades of the 1800s, New York State and a number of wealthy land speculators managed to gain control of all the Oneidas' territory save for thirty-two acres surrounding their ancestral village in Madison County. The legality of the treaties used to accomplish these land seizures remains contentious.[18]

As white settlement spread across central and western New York, the population of the Haudenosaunee people went into steep decline. Around 1650, when the Haudenosaunee were still relatively unaffected by European expansion, there were an estimated twenty-five thousand Iroquoian people, most of whom lived in what would become central and western New York. By 1850, the total Iroquoian population in all the United States and Canada had been reduced to approximately seven thousand. Although a small number of Haudenosaunee people still lived on what was once their home territory, most had been widely dispersed.[19]

One direct effect of this dramatic population shift was the removal of almost all Haudenosaunee access to the Adirondacks. Mohawk people who originally considered all of the eastern and central Adirondacks their exclusive territory became only occasional visitors. Oneida people who originally used the western portion including the Beaver River country were now so reduced and dispersed that their presence was eliminated. It is small wonder that Native people were seldom encountered when people of European ancestry first came to the central Adirondacks.

The fact that the Haudenosaunee population was much reduced does not mean it was gone entirely. Throughout the nineteenth century a small number of Mohawk and Abenaki people continued to live in the Adirondacks. Nineteenth-century Indigenous peoples did not live in traditional tribal communities; rather, they were scattered here and there throughout the region. They used their traditional skills in new ways to make a living among the new settlers. Many of the first pioneers to the region were helped and taught skills by the Haudenosaunee and Algonquian-speaking people already there. Native wilderness guides were praised for their skill. Mohawks helped build the Adirondack Division of the New York Central Railroad and worked in lumber camps. Until recently, this part of the story of Native American contributions to the region has been largely ignored. Melissa Otis's recent research, however, demonstrates an essentially unbroken occupation of the Adirondack region by Native Americans.[20]

One way in which the influence of Native American presence is still felt in the Adirondacks is through place names. Unfortunately, the words the Mohawk and Oneida people used to refer to the great north woods are not among them. Melissa Otis reminds us the Mohawks called the region *Tso-non-tes-ko-wa* (the mountains) or *Tsiio-non-tes-ko-wa* (the big mountains). The Oneidas called the region *Latilu-taks*, which translates as "they are eating the trees," a reference to the plentiful beaver in the Oneida territory of the north woods.[21]

The name for the region chosen by Prof. Ebenezer Emmons in his 1837 survey report to the New York legislature is a Mohawk word, but not their name for the region. Prof. Emmons reported he chose the name because he wanted to commemorate the name of the Native Americans that previously inhabited the area. Based on earlier published sources, Emmons incorrectly believed the term "Adirondacks" generally referred to all Algonquian tribes.[22] In the Mohawk language, certain bands of Algonquians who hunted in the eastern High Peaks area were called Rătīrōntăks. According to most sources, this term literally means "bark eaters'" or "porcupines." While this translation is widely accepted, the term can also be simply translated as "forest dwellers."[23]

There are few genuine Native American place names in the Beaver River country, most likely due to the absence of Haudenosaunee by the time outside settlers arrived. One notable exception derives from the name of the Beaver River itself. In the Mohawk language it is called Niiohehsà:ne.[24] When Dr. W. Seward Webb built his Great Camp at the headwaters of the Beaver River in 1893, he memorialized its original name by calling his domain Ne-Ha-Sa-Ne Park (see chapter 8 for more details on Nehasane Park).

# 2

# Claiming the Land

There were no recorded property titles to the millions of acres comprising New York's great north woods until just before the American Revolution. British colonial authorities in New York were generally of the opinion that the north woods were properly the territory of the nations of the Haudenosaunee.[1] Indian territory was not considered to be available for purchase.[2]

As settlement by people of European descent increased in the lowlands around the edges of the wild North Country, certain wealthy landowners saw an opportunity to obtain title to large tracts of what they saw as unoccupied land at a low price. They reasoned that immense profits would result if the land could be resold to other land speculators or to settlers moving into the frontier.

Three early North Country land speculation schemes involved the lands around the Beaver River. The land from the headwaters downstream to Grassy Point lies within the boundaries of the Totten and Crossfield Purchase. The remainder of the Beaver River country lies inside the Macomb Purchase: the land under and immediately around most of today's Stillwater Reservoir is made up parts of Townships Number Four and Number Five of John Brown's Tract, itself a smaller part of the Macomb Purchase.

By 1792, all of the Beaver River region had been claimed by land speculators. All of the property titles in the Beaver River region originate from these purchases. This chapter briefly discusses each of them in turn.

## The Totten and Crossfield Purchase

The earliest European formal purchase of land in the great northern wilderness occurred just prior to the Revolutionary War. The Totten and Crossfield Purchase of 1771 should not properly be called a purchase.[3] It was essentially a land swindle intended to formally remove control of a great portion of the north woods from the Mohawk Nation. The two named principals were not the actual purchasers, but straw men standing in for a group of wealthy land speculators. The real principal purchasers were brothers Edward and Ebenezer Jessup, along with a group of associates. The land speculators in collaboration with officials of the colony of New York paid selected chiefs of the Mohawk Nation a modest amount to sign a treaty with the British Crown that purportedly relinquished all Mohawk claims to about one quarter of the entire great north woods. The Crown then granted the land speculators title to a triangular wilderness tract of about 1,115,000 acres in return for a hefty fee.[4]

The Totten and Crossfield land speculators arranged to have the land they obtained surveyed and subdivided into fifty townships. Although this survey was never fully completed, it was the first attempt at a formal survey of any part of the Adirondacks and the first organized European exploration of a large part of it.[5] Native Americans familiar with the territory guided the surveyor, Archibald Campbell, until a dispute over payment caused Campbell's guides to quit.

The south line of the Totten and Crossfield Purchase traversed the Beaver River country slightly north of the present-day Grassy Point Road out of Beaver River Station, crossed the river, and continued on, passing close to Witchhopple Lake. The upper reaches of the Beaver River were inside the Totten and Crossfield Purchase, including the South Branch of the Beaver River, Little Rapids, Albany (now called Nehasane) Lake and Smith's Lake (now called Lake Lila). The comprehensive survey of Verplanck Colvin, begun a hundred years later in 1872, amazingly enough was able to retrace this line.[6]

The Jessups and their partners took possession of some of the new townships and began to sell the others. However, before all of the townships were sold, the colonies went to war with England. The Jessup brothers sided with the British, then fled to Canada at the war's end.

The victory of the colonies over England invalidated the Totten and Crossfield Purchase since the newly formed New York State seized the lands of all English loyalists, including the Jessup brothers. Some of the investors petitioned the New York state legislature to retain their titles, claiming they had supported the Revolution. Most of these petitions were successful, resulting in the state reaffirming title to those lands. The remainder of the Totten and Crossfield Purchase became the property of New York State and was later sold by the state land commission.

## The Macomb Purchase

One significant result of the success of the Revolution and the treaties that limited Native American land rights[7] was that New York suddenly found itself in possession of millions of acres of unsettled lands previously claimed by Native Americans, Loyalists, or the Crown. The state was also badly in need of funds due to expenditures during the American Revolution. Many in the state legislature saw sale of these new state lands as a quick way to raise necessary cash without raising taxes. Thus, on May 5, 1786, the New York state legislature created a state land commission charged with procuring speedy sale of all unoccupied state lands.

Influential land speculators argued that the law establishing the state land commission contained too many onerous restrictions limiting marketability. Accordingly, on March 22, 1791, the state legislature passed a new law that authorized the land commissioners to sell public lands "in such parcels, on such terms, and in such manner as they shall judge most conducive to the interest of the state."

Alexander Macomb was a member of the New York state legislature when the law authorizing state land sales was liberalized. He had a strong interest in land speculation, and some early success with it convinced him that that there was considerable money to be made by speculating in New York's northern wilderness lands. Because of his role as one of the silent investors in the earlier Totten and Crossfield Purchase, he also knew that there were few other investors willing to take such a risk and thus a very low price was likely.

5. Portrait of Alexander Macomb, photographic print mounted on mat board, uncredited photograph. Courtesy of the Burton Historical Collection, image bh007577, Detroit Public Library.

By 1791, the state still held title to almost four million acres of unoccupied land in in the North Country. In May, Macomb applied to the New York State land commission for the right to purchase 3,635,200 of these acres.[8] He offered to pay eight pence per acre, approximately twelve cents in today's money, or a total of about half a million dollars. Macomb's proposed purchase encompassed most of present-day St. Lawrence, Franklin, and Jefferson Counties, all of Lewis, and parts of Herkimer (where the Beaver River lay) and Oswego Counties. The land commission agreed to divide the area into six Great Tracts estimated to be about 640,000 acres each. Macomb was to receive a patent for each Great Tract as he tendered payment for that tract. Lacking other bids, the land commission approved Macomb's application on June 22, 1791.

Although Macomb and his backers were influential men of great wealth, some members of the state legislature were suspicious that the very low price of this massive land deal indicated the existence of illegal activity. The legislature held extensive hearings, but no wrongdoing was discovered. Known ever since as the Macomb Purchase, the

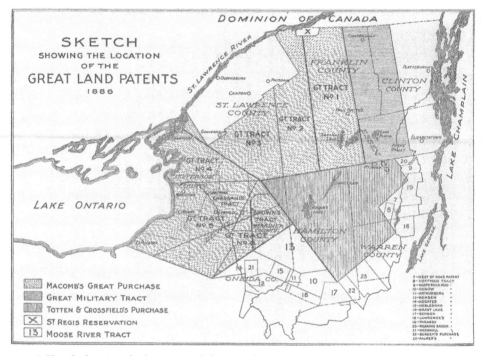

6. Sketch showing the locations of the great land patents, 1886. Donaldson, *History*, vol. 1, facing p. 52.

transaction remains the largest single land transfer in the state's history, comprising nearly one-eighth of the area of the entire state.[9]

By January 10, 1792, Macomb had raised enough money to obtain patents for Great Tracts IV, V, and VI. For a few months he held title to all of Jefferson and Lewis Counties as well as the northern half of Herkimer County. Macomb was never able to finalize purchase of the other three Great Tracts. His involvement in a questionable banking scheme soon left him deeply in debt. By the summer of 1792 Macomb was bankrupt and headed for debtor's prison. In order to preserve their investment, Macomb's silent partners, Daniel McCormick and William Constable, stepped in to complete the purchase.

Constable intended to use his many social and business contacts to sell large plots to other land speculators both in America and abroad. This plan immediately bore fruit. Only six months after obtaining

7. Gilbert Stuart (1755–1828), *William Kerin Constable*, 1796. Oil on canvas, 28 5/8 x 23 1/2 in. (72.7 x 59.7 cm). Bequest of Richard De Wolfe Brixey, 1943 (43.86.2). The Metropolitan Museum of Art, New York, NY, USA. Image copyright © The Metropolitan Museum of Art. Image source: Art Resource, NY.

title, he sold about half of this property to Samuel Ward, a banker, better than doubling his money in the process.[10] The upper Beaver River was included in this transaction.

### John Brown's Tract

Almost all of the land comprising the Macomb Purchase lay north or west of the Beaver River, except for the tract that William Constable sold to Samuel Ward. On November 25, 1794, Samuel Ward sold a significant parcel of the southeastern portion of his section of the Macomb Purchase, consisting of 210,000 acres, to James Greenleaf, son of a wealthy Boston merchant.[11] Unfortunately, during 1795 Greenleaf's financial dealings did not go well. In an attempt to meet his debts, on July 29, 1795, Greenleaf mortgaged these 210,000 acres of wilderness land to Philip Livingston, an influential New York merchant and a signer of the Declaration of Independence.

James Greenleaf was involved in a good deal more than land speculation. His commercial interests also included importing tea from China. His involvement in the tea trade brought him into contact with the Providence, Rhode Island, shipping firm of Brown & Francis. The partners in this firm were John Brown, one of the founders of Brown University, and John Francis, his son-in-law.

John Brown's long career as an entrepreneur, privateer, and China trade merchant made him one of the most prominent men in

Providence. Although he engaged in all forms of trade, his great wealth was built partly on the triangular trade, involving sale of African slaves and rum. His involvement in the slave trade caused considerable dissension within the Brown family. Moses Brown, his younger brother, became an abolitionist after converting to Quakerism later in life. John Brown, on the other hand, remained a defender of the slave trade, especially after he was elected to the US Congress in 1800.[12]

The way that John Brown obtained the Adirondack lands that still bear his name is complicated.[13] His business partner, John Francis, entered into a contract with James Greenleaf on July 30, 1795, to sell a warehouse full of tea, 420,000 pounds in all, for the sum of $157,500. Greenleaf paid for the tea with three promissory notes each for $52,500, payable in six, nine, and twelve months. As further security to guarantee payment of the third installment, John Francis was given a second mortgage on Greenleaf's Adirondack lands. Francis died on November 4, 1796, leaving the matter to be settled by his business partner, John Brown.

Over the next two years, John Brown tried unsuccessfully to collect on the Greenleaf promissory notes. By 1798, Brown concluded that the only way he would ever collect on the debt was to foreclose on his second mortgage and take possession of the Adirondack tract. Brown then learned that Philip Livingston had already reached the same conclusion and filed for foreclosure of his first mortgage the prior spring. Brown sought legal advice on this matter from Aaron Burr but later hired Alexander Hamilton to handle foreclosure of the Greenleaf mortgage. Hamilton was successful in negotiating with Livingston. On December 29, 1798, Brown became the sole owner of the 210,000 Adirondack acres that would come to be called John Brown's Tract.

Brown believed he would never see any profit from this purchase unless he could credibly claim the land was fit for settlement. He had the land surveyed and divided into eight townships, which he named for human virtues in hopes the names would attract conscientious settlers. Number 1 (Industry) was divided into 160-acre farms. Number 2 (Enterprise) and Number 3 (Perseverance) were divided into half-mile squares. The other townships were undivided. They are

Numbers 4 (Unanimity), 5 (Frugality), 6 (Sobriety), 7 (Economy), and 8 (Regularity). The Beaver River flows through the western portion of Brown's Tract in Townships Number 5 and Number 4.

Brown then built a rough frontier road north from Remsen to the boundary of Township Number Seven on the Moose River. In 1799, he built a small dam, a sawmill, and a gristmill at the site that would later become Old Forge. Unlike most previous land speculators, Brown actually visited his land, traveling at least as far as his mill. That was quite a feat for those days as Brown weighed about three hundred pounds and traveled over the rough wilderness roads using a specially designed carriage.

For the rest of his life Brown devised various methods to encourage settlement of Township Number Seven, but by the end of the eighteenth century all these plans had failed. The few settlers Brown lured to his mill left the area for better land elsewhere. His road gradually became overgrown. At the time of his death following a carriage accident on September 20, 1803, Brown had failed to start a permanent settlement anywhere on Brown's Tract.

The rest of the story of the spectacularly unsuccessful efforts to settle John Brown's Tract, first by John Brown's son-in-law, Charles Frederick Herreshoff, then by his grandsons, John Brown Francis and John Brown Herreshoff, is an epic tale. It is not further detailed here because it is peripheral to the story of the Beaver River.[14]

Even though land speculators had claimed the Beaver River region by the beginning of the nineteenth century, it remained pristine wilderness. The land speculators lived far away. There were no roads other than nearly forgotten foot trails of the Haudenosaunee. There were no settlers. In fact, settlers of European descent had only arrived at Lowville, New York, the town nearest the western edge of the Beaver River country, in 1798. For the time being the great forest remained undisturbed.

# 3

# Earliest Settlers

## The Pioneer Village of Number Four

The first settlement in the Beaver River country was in Township Number Four of John Brown's Tract. It owed its existence to the efforts of a grandson of John Brown, John Brown Francis.[1] After Francis inherited a part interest in John Brown's Tract, he decided to make new efforts to settle the property. The Beaver River in Township Number Four was about eighteen miles as the crow flies from the growing village of Lowville. In 1822, John Brown Francis financed the building of a road from the east side of the Black River just outside Lowville through the forest to the bank of the Beaver River, with the hope of selling lots to settlers. The location had promise, as the river was wide enough there to create a beautiful natural lake, soon to be named Beaver Lake.

To spur initial settlement, John Brown Francis offered one hundred acres free to each of the first ten families willing to clear the land and establish farms. Ten families responded to the offer and a pioneer village slowly started to take shape. By 1835 there were about seventy-five residents. For a few years Number Four even had its own school. But, after this hopeful start, the settlers gradually discovered that conditions at Number Four were not conducive to farming. The soil was thin and rocky. The winters were cold and long. Any potential market was a good distance away over a rough road. When W. Hudson Stephens visited the settlement of Number Four in 1864, it was nearly abandoned.

> An irregular winding road, through woods for eight miles, and we emerge amid partially cleared lands, with here and there an apple

8. John Nelson Arnold (1834–1909), *John Brown Francis*, 1881. Oil on canvas. Courtesy of the Brown University Portrait Collection.

and cherry tree in the grass plot of a deserted farm—into quite a "deserted village"—houses without tenants—barns wanting boards and crop—an abandoned school-house, windows out and door gone—into the cultivated clearing of No. 4. Beyond Chauncey Smith's on the left, and the Champlain Road, extending eighty miles into the Wilderness, on the right, the red house of Fenton, perched on brow of the hill, is approached by road leading down to Wetmore's, and through the lot to the landing on Beaver Lake.[2]

The only three pioneer families who remained at Number Four all made their living from the wilderness around them, not from farming. Chauncey Smith was a hunter, trapper, and wilderness guide, as was

Isaac Wetmore. The most successful of the early settlers was Orrin Fenton. His family settled in Number Four in 1826.[3] Fenton's first wife had recently died. One of the earlier settlers had the same last name as Fenton's first wife, so it may be that he moved there to be near family.[4] He and his second wife, Lucy Weller Fenton, devoted part of their farm to providing room and board to passing hunters and fishermen. In a few years the Fenton House had expanded to become a well-known sportsmen's hotel. A steady stream of sporting tourists who stayed at the Fenton homestead provided the family with a good living. (For more details about Fenton's, see chapter 7.)

The Number Four Road ended at the pioneer settlement. The only way farther east before the mid-1840s was by way of hunters' trails or by ascending the Beaver River. Although possible, travel eastward up the river from Beaver Lake was difficult.[5] The next ten miles of the Beaver River had no fewer than nineteen sets of unnavigable rapids and falls. For this reason, very few of the earliest visitors to Fenton's ventured very far upstream.[6]

To be sure, Number Four / Beaver Lake was and remains one of the most picturesque spots along the western edge of the Adirondacks. The deep forest and the views of the lake from Fenton's entranced early visitors. There was not only an admirable lake at the spot but also a number of beautiful falls nearby including High Falls, Fish Hole Falls, and Eagle Falls. The fishing and hunting were excellent. From its earliest days, Number Four seemed destined to become primarily a wilderness retreat, not an established village. Now, almost two hundred years later, modest summer cottages and camps dot the shores of Beaver Lake, but permanent dwellings are few and far between.[7]

### David Smith: ~1825–45

As noted, the rapids of the Beaver River east of Beaver Lake prevented most, but not all, upstream travel. A truly determined traveler could bypass the rapids and falls on foot trails, and some even did so carrying boats. After about ten arduous miles the steep river course through the forest opened up to a great marsh that stretched farther east for about eleven miles. The area above the falls was known at the time as the "still water" of the Beaver River.

All existing accounts agree that a man named David Smith was the earliest year-round inhabitant of the still water area. He is presumed to have arrived sometime in the 1820s and reportedly built a shanty near the junction of the Beaver River and Twitchell Creek.

Smith preferred the life of a hermit and did not welcome visitors. To avoid having his solitude interrupted by the infrequent hunter or trapper, sometime around 1830 Smith moved farther upstream where he cleared a few acres and built a cabin on the bank of the beautiful lake at the headwaters of the Beaver River. For many years thereafter that lake (now known as Lake Lila) was called Smith's Lake. We know that Smith was still living there in 1841 because the surveyor Nelson Beach employed Smith as a guide for a few days to assist in finding a course for the Carthage-to-Lake Champlain Road through the upper Beaver River area.[8] David Smith continued to live on the shore of the lake with his name until around 1845. He then disappeared.

There are no existing first-person accounts of Smith. Everything we know about him comes from stories handed down by local hunters, trappers, and guides. Nathaniel Bartlett Sylvester gave the earliest published account of Smith's life in 1877.[9] Sylvester claims that Smith lived by hunting and trapping and that he had an excellent collection of taxidermy specimens that he exhibited on his infrequent trips to town. Sylvester also describes an incident where Smith supposedly walked forty miles to Number Four in the dead of winter to get help because he was choking on a piece of moose meat. The highly unlikely taxidermy and choking stories seem exactly like the sort of tall tale guides might tell around the campfire.

Sylvester himself, ordinarily a careful chronicler of local history, seemed doubtful about the truth of the story he related about Smith's life. He openly mused about what the real Smith's life might be if it "could be written." Since Sylvester personally visited the Beaver River country on many occasions, he probably heard tales about David

Smith from several local residents, so he decided to tell Smith's story, whether all the details were true or not.

Later writers who bother to discuss the first settlement of the Beaver River country simply repeat some version of Sylvester's account of Smith's life.[10] One notable exception is the meticulously researched 1896 account of another attorney, Charles E. Snyder.[11] When discussing David Smith, Snyder explicitly notes that Smith was the subject of much speculation among local residents.

> The mystery of his life, no one so far as I have learned, has ever discovered. Some claim that he went to the woods on account of the death of his fiancée, others maintain that he sought refuge there because his wife made it too interesting for him at home, while still others insist that he was a political refugee from a foreign country, hiding here in the midst of the forest. All accounts of him agree that he was not a hunter and trapper. The deer, it is said, used to come about his place without fear.

Whether Sylvester's taxidermist or Snyder's deer-loving vegetarian was the real David Smith is impossible to know.[12] For now, the details of Smith's life remain mostly a guide's legend.

### James "Jimmy" O'Kane: 1844–58

Beginning in 1844, a wilderness road was cut across the Central Adirondacks from Carthage on the Black River to Crown Point on Lake Champlain. The road followed the Beaver River valley past the settlement of Number Four, avoided the rapids on a high esker a good distance back from the south bank of the river, and emerged from the forest at the west end of the still water. Even though it was not much more than a wide trail, the Carthage-to-Lake Champlain Road gave travelers much easier access to the upper sections of the Beaver River. (This road is more fully discussed in chapter 5.)

When the workers clearing the road reached the confluence of the Beaver River with Twitchell Creek at the still water, they built a log cabin on the high ground there to serve as temporary living quarters. Some time after the road builders left, a man named James O'Kane moved into the abandoned road builders' cabin. He lived there as a squatter until his death in January 1858.

We know quite a bit about O'Kane from firsthand reports. During a fishing and hunting trip in 1851 the artist Jervis McEntee and his friend Joseph Tubby spent the night in O'Kane's cabin.[13] McEntee described the cabin like this:

> Here is a specimen of what the seeker after the beautiful has to partake of by the way of accommodations. The cabin was built of logs having a bark roof and one window and door. It also possessed the luxury of a floor, a comfort that we shall not often meet, I fear, and last of all a large cooking stove.[14]

O'Kane himself did not make a favorable impression on the two young painters.

> He was tall, very tall, being six foot three inches, and although he stooped considerably, this was the first thing we remarked about him. He had long black hair and the unmistakable features of an Irishman and though we might have doubted from whence he came, these doubts were put to flight at the sound of his voice. Taking him altogether with his huge frame, his sunblossomed face, his old gray cravat and unctuous woolen shirt, he was decidedly an unpleasant-looking chap to sleep with in a log cabin.

McEntee admits that O'Kane tried to make them welcome, but stories told them by their guide led them to hide their liquor jug to keep O'Kane from using it too liberally. After an evening spent hunting, they all tried to get some sleep in the close, foul-smelling cabin. The two young artists remained uneasy.

> We turned in, however, and making pillows of our knapsacks and rolling ourselves in our blankets, sought sleep. The driver and Puffer [their guide] were soon unconscious, but with Jimmie's

soliloquies over the mice and chipmunks that ate his beans and the fears that if we all slept he might appropriate some of our small articles, kept Joe and I awake. However, after we had ceased answering his questions, for some time he laid down three or four old bags of straw, black with grease and dirt, and wrapped himself in an old blue military overcoat and amid mutterings and growls among which we could distinguish "Montreal and Quebec" he slid off into the quiet land.

We also have a first-person account from Sylvester, who visited O'Kane on at least several occasions during the 1850s.[15] Sylvester wrote that O'Kane grew his own vegetables to supplement what he could hunt or catch. Passing sportsmen contributed liberally to O'Kane's larder. Apparently, O'Kane kept a barrel of salted small animals in his cabin to eat in an emergency.[16]

O'Kane was also well known to the Constable family, who traveled along the Carthage-to-Lake Champlain Road several times during the 1850s on their way to Raquette Lake. They described him as "a miserable specimen of humanity, who, according to his own account, has been living at this spot for the past seven years, in a wretched shanty, with no companion but a dog."[17]

When Sylvester visited in May 1857, he found O'Kane feeble and ill, noting, "It was the first day of the spring in which he had been able to crawl out to the bridge across the creek and set his poles for fishing." O'Kane died the following January. He was the first person on record to be buried at Stillwater, supposedly at his favorite spot on the high bank of Twitchell Creek.[18]

There was no new settlement in the Beaver River country beyond Number Four until around 1870, when William Wardwell moved his family to Stillwater. The Carthage-to-Lake Champlain Road, cut through between 1844 and 1850, was little used. Lumbering came to the region in the 1850s; lumber camps were built and abandoned in a number of places along the course of the river. A few market hunters and trappers based at Number Four built shanties or rough cabins in one or two spots. Visiting sportsmen erected a semipermanent camp or two at Albany Lake and Smith's Lake. Otherwise, from the time of the first road was cut to Number Four in 1822 until the end of the Civil War, the Beaver River country remained essentially untouched by civilization.

# Part Two

# Early Tourists

9. An old-time sanitarium, Stillwater on the Beaver River, uncredited photograph. *Eighth and Ninth Reports of the Forest, Fish and Game Commission (1902–1903),* facing p. 278.

# 4

# The Red Horse Trail

### Origins of the Trail

Foot trails known to the Haudenosaunee traversed the Beaver River country long before the first white settlers arrived. There is no record of the exact location of these trails or even of how many trails there were. The first account of a person of European descent crossing the region on foot is in the diary of French Jesuit Priest Joseph Poncet.[1] A band of Mohawks took Father Poncet captive in Canada in August 1653. The band forced Poncet to accompany them as they traveled south to their village in the Mohawk River Valley. Based on his description of the journey, their route likely crossed the upper Beaver River.[2] One hundred and twenty-four years later, Mohawk guides led Sir John Johnson and his band of Loyalist troops in their flight to Canada in May 1776. In order to avoid the most common routes they ascended the Sacandaga River, passed by Raquette Lake, and traveled on northwest to the St. Lawrence River, crossing the Beaver River.[3]

Both of these early accounts strongly suggest the long-term existence of at least one trail known to the Mohawks that crossed the great north woods in a northwesterly direction from the Mohawk River, passing in the vicinity of Raquette Lake and then across Beaver River on the way to the St. Lawrence. There are few places where such a trail might leave the Beaver River Valley to cross the ridge to the north-flowing Oswegatchie River. The most obvious choice would be to follow the course of Red Horse Creek, which drains lands north of the Beaver River toward the divide with the Oswegatchie watershed.

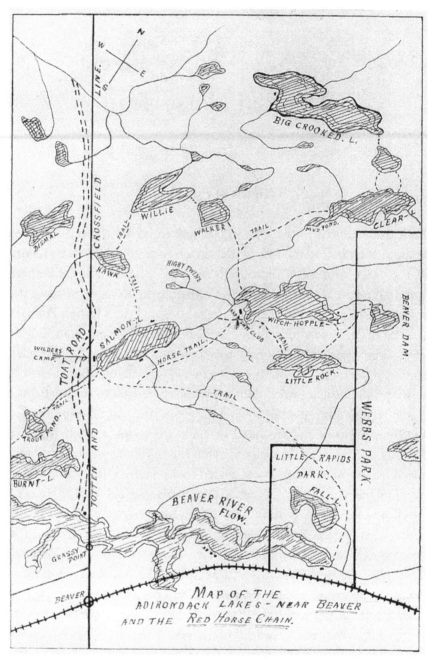

10. Postcard map of Red Horse Chain of Lakes, undated postcard map, creator unknown. Courtesy of Dennis Buckley.

By the time the first people of European descent pushed into the Beaver River country in the decades before the Civil War, the Haudenosaunee were gone but traces of an old established trail still existed along Red Horse Creek and on to the north. The hunters, trappers, and fishermen who first explored the upper Beaver River rediscovered the trail. They opened a number of side trails to the lakes and ponds in the vicinity and they built crude shanties for shelter that were frequently used by early sporting tourists.[4]

The first published account of the Red Horse Trail was in Edwin R. Wallace's 1872 edition of his *Descriptive Guide to the Adirondacks*.[5] Wallace highly recommended the Red Horse Chain of Lakes, especially for its superior fishing. He continued to feature the trail in successive editions of his *Guide*, with each edition providing more details. In his 1888 edition he explained that the creek was named for the red horse sucker fish that were once abundant in one of the lakes on the chain. Wallace's guides were popular, and for the remainder of the nineteenth century ever-increasing numbers of sporting tourists and their guides made use of the trail.

For most of the nineteenth century, Red Horse Creek emptied directly into the Beaver River from the north about five miles downstream from the foot of Little Rapids. It is a modest, shallow stream, easily overlooked, but it drains a series of beautiful natural glacial lakes and ponds. Ascending the creek, the traveler arrives in turn at Big Burnt Lake, Trout Pond, Salmon Lake, and Witchhopple Lake. Three small streams flow into Witchhopple Lake. The westernmost, near the outlet, drops in from Clear Lake. The next to the east drains Negro Lake, while the one farthest east flows in across a beaver meadow from Beaver Dam Pond and Wilder Pond. There are at least half a dozen other small lakes and ponds in the immediate vicinity. All along the way the Red Horse Trail passes through miles of spectacular old-growth forest.

## The Improved Trail

The trail was not much improved until the state purchased the land surrounding the Red Horse Chain in 1896. The state acquired almost

11. On the carry, outlet of Salmon Lake (Webb Purchase), photograph by F. J. Severance. *Second Annual Report of the Commissioners of Fisheries, Game and Forests*, facing p. 376.

seventy-five thousand acres of virgin forest in order to settle a lawsuit brought by the landowner, Dr. William Seward Webb. The details of this purchase are described in chapter 6. Part of the settlement required Dr. Webb to bear the expense of clearing and extending the existing Red Horse Trail. This benefited Webb because he wanted to keep users of the new public state land away from his adjoining Great Camp, Nehasane Park.

The improvements were made in early 1896 under the supervision of Webb's superintendent, Fitz Greene Hallock. The Red Horse Trail was marked and widened to make it suitable for use as a guideboat carry as far as Big Crooked Lake. Beyond Big Crooked, the original trail was cleared of brush and marked to an intersection with the abandoned 1815 Albany Road north of Gull Lake where a still-discernable

12. On the trail to Witchhopple, uncredited gelatin silver print from the Robert Gillespie photo album, captioned below, "Inlet of Salmon Lake—Where the Big Frogs Live / On the Trail to Witch-Hopple." ADKX #P074216, Catalog #2006.063.0001y. Courtesy of the Adirondack Experience.

path led to the High Falls of the Oswegatchie River. (For more on the Albany Road, see chapter 5.)

The earliest USGS maps clearly show the Red Horse Trail. Specifically, the Big Moose Quadrangle of 1903 shows the section from the Beaver River to a short distance north of Crooked Lake.[6] The first edition of the Cranberry Lake Quadrangle shows the north end of the trail from Crooked Lake to Sliding Falls on the Robinson River, then to the Oswegatchie River at High Falls.

In 1901, the Rap-Shaw Fishing and Hunting Club built its camp at the foot of Witchhopple Lake, right along the Red Horse Trail. Club members and guides maintained the main trail and cleared side trails to favored lakes in the area, placing boats at strategic spots on all the main lakes. Even after the Rap-Shaw Club moved their headquarters to Beaver Dam Pond, they continued to maintain all these trails. (For more on this club, see chapter 12.)

The illustrated diary of Bob Gillespie contains an amusing description of the trail as it existed in August 1919.[7] Gillespie often camped with friends at Salmon Lake along the Red Horse Chain. It took him and his companions only half a day to hike from camp to the High Falls of the Oswegatchie. Along the way they explored the ruins of the old Fur, Fins, and Feathers Camp near Sliding Falls on the Robinson River. At High Falls they encountered about twenty people camping in half a dozen old cabins. They slept in an unoccupied leaky cabin and hiked back to Salmon Lake the next morning.[8]

### Later Improvements, Abandonment, and Recovery

Paul Jamieson in *Adirondack Canoe Waters–North Flow* notes that around 1919 the Red Horse Trail was improved by the State Conservation Commission with the aid of R. K. Jessup, one of the founders of the Adirondack Mountain Club.[9] This may have included building a bridge across the Oswegatchie near High Falls, upgrading the existing trail, and installing new trail markers.[10]

The Red Horse Trail was used fairly heavily through the early twentieth century. Until the state evicted the many squatters from the Forest Preserve in 1916, at least six substantial guide's camps catered to visitors in the vicinity of the south end of the trail.[11] The Rap-Shaw Club, with one hundred members and an equal number of guests, continued to use the trail frequently until 1939, when their camp at Beaver Dam Pond burned.

The trail was popular in those days because it was fairly easy to reach by public transportation. Passenger rail service to Beaver River Station started in 1892. By 1900 a fine hotel next to the train station, the Norridgewock, catered to campers, hikers, hunters, and fishermen. From there it was easy to hire a guide to transport gear to any location along the Red Horse Chain. As discussed in chapter 8, a dam at Stillwater, completed in 1925, created a reservoir that flooded access to the trail, but a good number of people still visited the area by crossing from Grassy Point near Beaver River Station using boats equipped with newly popular outboard motors.

Visitation declined steeply after World War II with the rise of the automobile. Finally, in 1964, scheduled passenger train service to Beaver River Station ended. Because the trail is located so far from the nearest road, use of the Red Horse Trail nearly stopped. By the time Stillwater Reservoir had a full-time forest ranger in 1967, the Red Horse Trail had faded into obscurity.

As camping, fishing, and boating became more popular on the reservoir after 1980, the local DEC ranger, Terry Perkins, set about restoring the trail. He replaced the rotted footbridges and personally hiked the whole distance to High Falls to clear brush and replace trail markers. Unfortunately, in July 1995 a crippling windstorm produced widespread blowdown that obliterated the trail north of Crooked Lake.[12] The DEC now maintains the trail only from Trout Pond, now a bay of the Stillwater Reservoir, as far as Clear Lake.

It is still possible to hike the southern section of this beautiful and historic trail. The trailhead is located along the north shore of the reservoir about five miles east of the state boat launch. Hikers must bring their own boat or use the water taxi service available from the Norridgewock Lodge in Beaver River. The trail begins at the east end of Trout Pond. The outlet of Trout Pond can be difficult to find in low water so it is best to carry a map and consult a knowledgeable local before setting out. There is a DEC lean-to at the northeast end of Trout Pond where the trail begins.[13]

# 5

# The Road to Stillwater

Long-distance travel in the North Country during the nineteenth century required roads suitable for horse and wagon. As noted previously, North Country land speculators such as John Brown and William Constable understood that financing road-building was part of the cost of wilderness land sales. John Brown Francis, grandson of John Brown, paid for clearing a wagon road from the Black River valley to Beaver Lake in Township Number Four on the western edge of the Beaver River country because he knew he would not be able to sell plots of land to settlers without a road to the nearest town.[1] That road, built in 1822, was called then, as it is now, the Number Four Road, and followed essentially the same route the Number Four Road uses today.

## The Albany Road

The Number Four Road was not the first road into the Beaver River country. On June 19, 1812, the New York state legislature authorized "opening and making a road between the City of Albany and the river St. Lawrence." There was already a road from Albany as far as Fish House on the Sacandaga River. The Albany Road started at Fish House and ran diagonally northwest across the wilderness. It passed near Raquette Lake and crossed the Beaver River on a bridge over a narrow section of Albany (now Nehasane) Lake. It continued north, crossed the Oswegatchie River near High Falls, then connected to the St. Lawrence Turnpike about ten miles south of the village of Russell. The Albany Road was completed to the vicinity of Russell in 1815. As noted in the last chapter, part of the road followed an old

Haudenosaunee trail across the wilderness, likely the same trail used in 1776 by Sir John Johnson in his retreat to Canada.[2]

The Albany Road can be clearly seen on the 1818 *Map of the State of New York with Parts of Adjacent States* by John H. Eddy and on John Richard's map of 1821. It had a very short useful existence.[3] Despite what the state legislature may have believed when it authorized the Albany Road, there was very little need for it. Because most of the road was never maintained, the forest quickly returned and it became impassable. Some evidence of its existence persisted long after it ceased to be traveled. For example, parts of the rotting bridge over the Beaver River at Albany Lake and a faint trace of the road could still be seen in 1851.[4]

There are some who persist in calling the Albany Road a military road connected in some vague way to the War of 1812. There is scant evidence to support this surmise. The Albany Road was not completed until three years after the end of the War of 1812 and there are no credible accounts of it ever being used by troops.[5] The St. Lawrence Turnpike was used to move supplies and troops during the War of 1812. Since the Albany Road eventually connected to the St. Lawrence Turnpike, it may have obtained its military connotation by loose association.

### The Carthage-to-Lake Champlain Road

There was no further road-building activity in the Beaver River country until 1841, when the New York state legislature authorized construction of a road all the way across the Central Adirondacks from west to east. Because this road started at Carthage on the Black River and ended at Crown Point on Lake Champlain it was named the Carthage-to-Lake Champlain Road. In some accounts it was called the Catamount Road or simply the State Road. It roughly followed the Beaver River valley from the Black River upstream, passing near the settlement of Number Four and skirting the next ten miles of rapids upstream before arriving back at the Beaver River at Stillwater. It crossed Twitchell Creek on a rickety log bridge and continued up

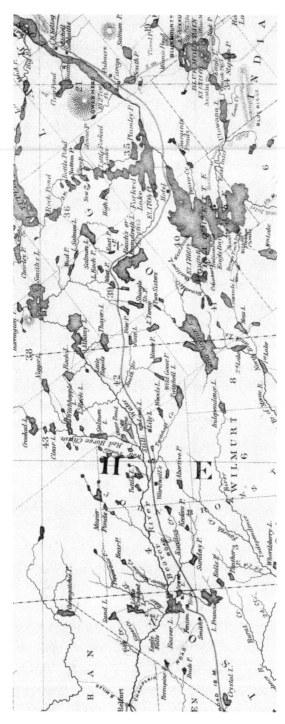

13. Detail from *Map of the New York Wilderness* by W. W. Ely showing the Carthage-to-Lake Champlain Road from Number Four to Long Lake. Wallace, *Guide.*

the south side of the river to near Little Rapids before turning toward Raquette Lake.[6] The current gravel road from Number Four to Stillwater follows the course of this original road with only one minor deviation.

The Carthage-to-Lake Champlain Road was laid out and built in sections primarily by Nelson J. Beach of Lewis County along with David Judd in Essex County and Nathan Ingerson in Jefferson County.[7] The expense of building and maintaining the road was to be defrayed by a tax on the nonresident lands to be benefitted. The road was surveyed in the summer of 1841 and opened in sections over the next ten years.[8] The road reached the confluence of the Beaver River with Twitchell Creek at the still water by the fall of 1844.[9] Twitchell Creek proved to be a major obstacle. It took the road-builders quite some time to construct a log wagon bridge at the spot. While working on the bridge they built a small log cabin as a way station.[10]

This wilderness road was not much more than a wide trail through the forest. Trees were felled and stumps removed when possible. Superficial rocks were thrown into the woods but larger embedded rocks stayed put. Marshy spots and shallow streams were crossed on "corduroy," small logs placed side by side perpendicular to the direction of travel. Deeper or wider streams merited crude log bridges.

Most of the road was complete by around 1850. Unfortunately, the planned taxation on nonresidents did not yield adequate funds to maintain it. Local residents maintained some sections.[11] The more remote sections slowly became impassable as bridges and corduroy rotted. In 1872 the state legislature appropriated modest funds to repair parts of the road. The state made no further efforts to maintain it in its entirety.[12]

As with the Albany Road, there is a mistaken but persistent belief that some or all of the Carthage-to-Lake Champlain Road followed the course of an old "military road" connected in some way to the War of 1812.[13] There is no evidence this was the case.[14] The earliest published accounts of the Beaver River country, such as Stephens's *Historical Notes* and Snyder's "John Brown's Tract," do not mention any road through the area predating the 1822 Number Four Road and the

1844 Carthage-to-Lake Champlain Road. Donaldson devotes a short chapter in his *History* to so-called Old Military Roads in which he describes every documented 1812-vintage road.[15] None crossed the central Adirondacks from west to east.[16]

Some of the confusion about the Carthage-to-Lake Champlain Road being a military road may stem from nineteenth-century maps that appear to indicate that it coexisted with the old Albany Road and that they intersected just south of Beaver River near Albany Mountain.[17] While this may seem to give both roads a plausible military use as a route to the St. Lawrence River Valley, in fact they never coexisted.[18]

## Traveling the Road

In March 1851, Dr. Benjamin Brandreth, manufacturer of a popular patent medicine, bought all of Township Thirty-Nine of the Totten and Crossfield Purchase. His property lay just south of the upper Beaver River. At that time the Carthage-to-Lake Champlain Road crossed Township Thirty-Nine from Little Rapids on the Beaver River in the north to Raquette Lake on the south. In fact, the existence of the road was probably one of the reasons that Brandreth chose to buy the property.[19] Brandreth assumed there would be travelers on the road and tried to make them feel welcome. He opened a log cabin near Brandreth (formerly Beach's) Lake to visitors and sometimes lent them a boat or even a horse. The guestbook from the Brandreth cabin has numerous travelers' entries from 1851 up through 1882.[20]

Even in the early days the section of the road between Number Four and Raquette Lake received little maintenance. When the artist Jervis McEntee traveled through the Beaver River Country in 1851, he preferred to use a boat when possible, rather than the road. He described the road as:

> . . . simply a path through the woods, with an attempt at bridging streams and morasses with corduroy, and [that] was opened with a view of inducing settlers to go in and occupy the lands through which it runs. It has had but little effect in this way, however, and

seems practically useless, as there are often whole years during which it is not traveled by a single team throughout its entire length. Fishing and hunting parties frequently avail themselves of it in hauling their provisions to Raquette Lake, but the labor of traveling it is more than many care to undergo.[21]

The intrepid Constable family took Adirondack camping trips in 1850, 1851, and 1855 by driving their wagons across the western portion of the road from Number Four to Raquette Lake.[22] Even as early as 1850, the same year the road was completed, it was in terrible condition, full of mud holes, rocks, and fallen trees. Walking was usually much more comfortable than riding. John Constable described the challenges posed by the road as follows:

We had a balky horse who would either not go at all, or else with such a rush as to stave everything to pieces over the rocks and gullies which constituted our road . . . it required the greatest care and skill to keep our only team from smashing the wagon to pieces. The teamster walked behind to pick up the articles that were constantly thrown off by the violent jerks . . . which frequently came near plunging me headlong into the bushes.[23]

By the mid-1870s, the section from Number Four to Stillwater was reduced to a path generally not fit for travel by wagon.[24] Nonetheless, there were some who tried. Charles Fenton, renowned guide and owner of the Fenton House at Number Four, took a group of sportsmen over most of the road in 1875. Their road adventure is worth retelling at some length.

After five days of bouncing over the Catamount or Carthage Road in a wagon containing supplies for two months' hunt, we finally reached the little hamlet of Pendleton [now Newcomb] where lived four or five families. The road had been given up as impassable several years before so we asked a grave-looking man what our chances were of getting over it. He shook his head doubtfully. Then we turned to our teamster.

"Well," quoth he, "I hev druv this here old team in the woods for 20 years and I hev never seed anyplace so bad that I couldn't git through somehow!" And so, we moved on and that our faith in him was well-founded is [was] soon proved.

The "road" continued to get progressively worse so we finally came to a place where the corduroy was all broken up and the mud holes seemed unfathomable. Our party was walking some distance ahead and, wishing to see how our doughty driver would handle the situation, we hid in a roadside thicket and watched. Well, as soon as he came to the quagmire he stopped, scanned the scene, glanced ahead to see if we were still in sight, then settled back on his seat, took a firm grip on the reins—and plunged in.

Down, down went the horses into the muck and broken logs, he swinging his whip lustily and loudly urging on his trusty and trusting steeds. No use. They floundered around until they made it about to the middle of the mess, then one became so entangled that it fell over on its side. The poor beast put out its utmost effort but it only got itself bogged down even deeper.

In the meantime, our dauntless driver seemed not in the least discouraged. He simply dismounted, patted his horse on the head, told it to take it easy and that he would soon be back to help him. He then sat nonchalantly down on a log, pulled out his pipe, charged it and started puffing away as though he hadn't a care in the world.

After a while he got his axe from the wagon, cut a stout pole to use as a lever, adjusted a fulcrum, ran his lever under the horse's belly and started prying him up.

At this turn of affairs, we could hold out no longer so revealed ourselves by uproarious laughter. Then we went to the rescue, helped extricate the critters and proceeded on our way, rejoicing.[25]

## The End of the Road

Lack of use, nonexistent maintenance, and the regenerative power of the great northern forest slowly turned much of the Carthage-to-Lake Champlain Road into no more than a barely discernable footpath. By the end of the 1880s only selected sections of the road were still passable. The *Report of the Forest Commission for 1891* characterized most of the road as "a mere string of rocks and mud holes."[26] Wallace's *Guide*, 1894 edition, reported that many western portions could not be traveled by wagons, especially from Belfort to Number Four and from Little Rapids to Brandreth. By 1897, Wallace's *Guide* reported that the road through Brandreth Park was completely closed.[27]

Even though it was rough, the section of the road between Number Four and Stillwater received a fair amount of use prior to 1890. In those days the Beaver River country was a magnet for many outdoors enthusiasts. As will be detailed in the following chapters, during this time sportsmen's hotels prospered at Number Four (Fenton's), Stillwater (Dunbar's), Little Rapids (Muncy's) and Smith's Lake (Lamont's). Everyone bound for the upper Beaver River needed to use that section of the road to bypass the impassable rapids on the river.

The road between Number Four and Stillwater took on new life in October 1892 with the opening of the railroad. Although tourists visiting the area now commonly came by train, a good many of the growing number of folks who worked in the woods or at the new hotels used the road. Because of the increased commercial activity around the community of Beaver River Station, the section of the Carthage-to-Lake Champlain Road between there and Number Four actually received increased traffic after 1892, resulting in gradual improvements.

The biggest problem in using the road beyond Stillwater to the east was the condition of the bridge over Twitchell Creek. When Nelson Beach originally laid out the Carthage-to-Lake Champlain Road in 1841, he spent several days searching for a way around Twitchell Creek. Only after all the other possibilities had been exhausted did he decide on a route that required a bridge.[28]

From the beginning, the Twitchell Creek bridge proved hard to maintain. The original 1844 bridge was built of logs balanced on piers of rock. As early as 1855, crossing the bridge with a wagon and team was precarious.[29] Records are not clear on how long the first bridge remained passable. Suffice it to say, most early travelers left the road at Stillwater and ascended the next section of the river by boat.[30] Doubtless the bridge was repaired from time to time over the next thirty

14. Bridge and Club House, Beaver River, New York, Twitchell Creek bridge looking back at the Beaver River Club, undated photo postcard attributed to Henry M.
Beach, Rap-Shaw Photo Album image 1-25. Courtesy of the Rap-Shaw Club, Inc.

years by those who absolutely needed to get a wagonload of goods
across the creek.

The series of impoundment dams built on the Beaver River repeatedly destroyed the bridge. (Chapter 8 provides details on the Beaver
River dams.) Higher water behind the dam of 1887 totally washed
away the old Twitchell Creek log bridge. A. J. Muncy, who regularly
used the road to get supplies from Lowville to his sportsmen's hotel at
Little Rapids, reported that in order to keep using the road he had to
build a floating bridge in one place and use a ferryboat in another to
cross with his team.[31]

The second dam, completed in 1894, again widened Twitchell
Creek. A group of upstate businessmen had just purchased two hundred acres and the Dunbar Hotel near the projected dam to create the
Beaver River Club, a private sportsmen's preserve. (See chapter 11.) The
new dam turned their property into a two-hundred-acre island. Members and guests of the Beaver River Club arrived by train, then took a

15. Twitchell Creek Bridge destroyed by ice, 1911, uncredited photograph from the Churchill-Shaver Album. Courtesy of Jim and Carol Fox.

small private steamer down the river to their clubhouse. They needed to restore the Twitchell Creek bridge because they hauled luggage and other heavy goods by wagon from the railroad station to the club.

Accordingly, they used their combined political influence to get the state legislature to appropriate funds for a new bridge.[32] The new bridge needed to be much longer, so the bridge was built in two sections. The first span crossed to a small island in the creek. A much longer span was built on the other side of the "road island." The club also constructed a low bridge on the west side of their property over the enlarged Alder Creek, previously crossed at a ford. A third low bridge crossed an inlet of the Flow near the clubhouse.

When the 1902–3 concrete dam replaced the 1894 dam, the water level was not much changed, so new bridges were not necessary. The bridge across Twitchell Creek built in 1894 was replaced with a new structure during the winter of 1909–10.[33] During the winter of 1911, shifting ice displaced the new piers, destroying the longest span. Crossing to the six-mile-long section of the road leading to the railroad station again required use of a ferry. There is no evidence that the Twitchell Creek bridge was replaced after 1911.[34]

Even with the road cut off at Twitchell Creek, it remained in use from Number Four as far as Stillwater to serve the Beaver River Club and the adjacent Old Homestead / Beaver River Inn. The creation of the current Stillwater Reservoir in 1924 raised the water level another nineteen feet, completely flooding the Beaver River Club property. Since that time the road has ended at the water's edge in the hamlet of Stillwater.[35]

# 6

# Sporting Tourists Arrive

## A New Use for Wilderness

The early Adirondack settlers who stayed long enough to put down roots had to find ways to make a living from the wilderness. The land was not suited for anything more than subsistence agriculture.[1] Out of necessity they became skilled at using the resources provided by the forest. Like the Native Americans who came before them, they scouted the forest for fish and game. Some found they could make a modest living by trapping and market hunting.

Then, ever so gradually, a trickle of tourists began to find their way into the great north woods. The settlers found that catering to tourists provided them with a new source of income. Enterprising men with knowledge of the woods started to work as wilderness guides along the routes commonly used by tourists while their wives converted part of the homestead into a basic sportsmen's hotel.

Adirondack sporting tourism developed during the first half of the nineteenth century in response to increased industrialization and urbanization. Urban Americans still thought of themselves as rugged and self-reliant, but there were fewer and fewer opportunities to exercise these traits. The romance of surviving in the untracked wilderness by hunting and fishing became a common, mostly male, fantasy.

Of course, humans had fished and hunted for subsistence for millennia, but hunting and fishing for sport was a relatively new development. Fishing for sport became popular in Europe only in the seventeenth century,[2] but was restricted primarily to the wealthy until the advent of mass-produced fishing gear in the mid-nineteenth century. Fishing for sport, especially fly-fishing, became popular in America about the same time as it did in Europe, for the same reason.[3] Hunting for sport also became popular in the mid-nineteenth century, with the invention of rifles using cartridges. The introduction of the Spencer repeating carbine in 1860 and the Winchester rifle in 1873 made hunting feasible for amateur sportsmen.

At first, tourists from the cities ventured only to the edges of the Adirondack wilderness where the earliest sportsmen's hotels were located. Sporting tourists ventured farther and farther afield as new routes into the interior were established.

Most of the earliest sporting tourists were men, but women were also commonly seen in the backcountry. Writing in 1849, Joel Headley remarked that a quarter of a century earlier, "the idea of a lady visiting [the Adirondacks] for pleasure never entered the head of anyone. Now ladies go in crowds."[4] Headley was aware that many women enjoyed camping out. "One class goes to the woods to rough it like any man. They like the tent life—the distant exploration and the hunter's fare and sometimes use his rifle or the sportsmen's rod."[5]

As camping, fishing, and hunting became more and more popular with urbanites, magazines and newspapers responded by publishing stories extolling the virtues of outdoor life. In 1840, William Porter, editor of *Spirit of the Times*, a leading magazine, published an article praising the wonderful fishing and hunting during his visit to the Central Adirondacks. Headley's *The Adirondack; or, Life in the Woods* (1849), was the first book-length account of the advantages of an extended vacation in New York's northern wilderness. The most popular of all nineteenth-century Adirondack adventure books, William Henry Harrison Murray's *Adventures in the Wilderness; or, Camp-life in the Adirondacks*, was published in 1869. A veritable flood of wilderness tourism followed.

## Notable Early Tourists

There are reliable records of sporting tourists crossing the Beaver River country at least as early as 1836.[6] By the 1850s, summer sporting tourism had become commonplace. The attractions that drew them were the renowned beauty of Smith's Lake at the head of the Beaver River and the unequalled bounty of deer and trout.

Trips of those days typically lasted for a month or more. Tourists required guides to do the heavy work. The weight of the boats, gear, and supplies hauled through the backcountry nearly defies imagination.

A fair sense of those days can be found in the meticulous records of the outdoor exploits of four notable early Beaver River country tourists.

*The Constable Family Camping Trips (1850–55)*

William Constable Sr. once held title to most of the Adirondacks, but he never set foot in the region. When his son William Jr. took over the task of managing and selling the remaining property, he decided to build the family a country manor house, which they christened Constable Hall, overlooking the Black River valley near Turin.

In 1819, while supervising construction of Constable Hall, a ten-ton capstone fell on William Jr. He never fully recovered and died two years later in 1821. His thirty-three-year-old widow, Mary Eliza McVickar Constable, inherited the property.

William Jr. and Mary Eliza had five children, four boys and a girl: William III, aka Will (1811–87), John III (1813–87), James (1814–92), Stevenson (1816–94), and Anna (1820–1906). All the children were educated at home until they were teenagers, then the boys were sent to Europe for a classical secondary education. Their summers were spent exploring the countryside around Constable Hall.

John Constable seemed to be particularly attracted to the outdoors. His first trip into the Adirondacks was to Fourth Lake in 1833. One or more of his brothers probably accompanied him on that trip. He enjoyed the experience so much that he and his brothers took frequent camping trips into the Central Adirondacks for the next decade.[7] He took a particularly ambitious trip in 1836 with his brother Stevenson and a friend, Casimir De Rham. Leaving from Old Forge they paddled up the Fulton Chain, made a series of carries to reach as far as Tupper Lake, and returned via Raquette Lake, Big Moose Lake, Smith's Lake, then out down the Beaver River.[8]

It is likely, however, that the idea for the first Constable family camping trip came from Anna Constable. She grew up listening to her older brothers rave about the Adirondacks in general, and Raquette Lake in particular. When she learned her brothers were planning another trip to Raquette Lake in 1850, she wanted to go along. The first family camping trip was a success, so the siblings agreed to repeat the journey in 1851 and 1855.

The campers probably traveled in two carriages for the first day of the trip along decent roads from Constable Hall to Lowville, thence across the Black River and along the Number Four Road to Fenton's, where they had dinner and spent the night. The first day's trip covered about thirty-five miles.

Early the next morning, they left Fenton's on the Carthage-to-Lake Champlain Road. One carriage was sent back. Owing to the terrible condition of the road, most of the party walked almost all of the way. By about noon they reached the log bridge across Twitchell Creek at Stillwater. The bridge was so precarious they had to walk their horses across with the help of the hermit Jimmy O'Kane, whose cabin was right by the bridge.

As they hurried to reach their second night's camp at the foot of Albany Mountain, it started to rain; then an axle on their supply wagon broke. They were greatly relieved that the axle could be repaired using materials at hand. The second day's journey totaled about twenty-three miles and took from dawn until after dark. They covered the remaining twelve miles to the shores of Raquette Lake during the first part of the third day. Their two brothers and the guides were waiting to row them five miles across the lake to Sand Point, where the recently completed open camps were ready.

Even though these family camping trips involved considerable exertion and rough conditions, it was the consensus that they were a lot of fun and good for everybody's health. As "Bob Racket" put it,

> It was productive not only of a vast deal of enjoyment to all the party,
> but conduced wonderfully to their health, especially of the ladies, who
> gained so much weight as scarcely to be recognized by their friends.[9]

### *Jervis McEntee (1851)*

Jervis McEntee was born in 1828 in Rondout, New York, near Kingston. Little is known about his early life except that he attended the Clinton Liberal Institute from 1844 to 1846.[10] On leaving school, he devoted himself to landscape painting. By 1851 he was accomplished enough to become an apprentice to Frederic Edwin Church, leader of the Hudson River School of landscape painting. During the early summer of 1851, McEntee and his artist friend, Joseph Tubby, made an extended trek across the Adirondacks guided by Asa Puffer. McEntee kept a detailed journal of the trip that began with a three-week sojourn in the Beaver River country.[11]

16. Jervis McEntee, Albumen silver print, Sarony & Co. (~1870–75). Courtesy of J. Paul Getty Museum, Object no. 84.XD.1157.1613.

In a magazine article McEntee published in 1859, he says he and his friend traveled to Rome on the Erie Canal, then took a stagecoach to Lowville, the starting point for their wilderness trip.[12] They left Lowville early on the morning of June 12, 1851, traveling up the Number Four Road in a wagon. They arrived at Orrin and Lucy Fenton's homestead at Number Four late in the morning. They had a good dinner (the midday meal) at Fenton's and fed the horses.

As soon as they finished eating, they left for Stillwater. The road was so rough that they walked behind the wagon most of the way. It took them all afternoon to reach their destination. They arrived at

O'Kane's log cabin at the Twitchell Creek bridge about sunset. The cabin had a bark roof, one window, one door, and the "luxury" of a floor.[13] Puffer made them dinner consisting of venison with salt pork, a pigeon McEntee had shot earlier in the day, crackers, and black tea. They went jacklighting for deer that night and although they stayed out until midnight, they did not get a deer.

The next morning, they were unable to find the boat they intended to use, so they borrowed a boat from O'Kane and set out up the Beaver River. After rowing leisurely all day and carrying their gear around a log jam, they reached a spot where Puffer said there was a nearby shanty. They hiked a way back into the woods and found a shanty built against a large rock.[14] McEntee noted that the black flies (he called them punkies) were very bad. The hut where they spent the night was ten feet square with a two-foot square hole for a door and a hole in the roof to let the smoke out.

They reached the South Branch of the Beaver River about noon the next day. They expected to stay at a shanty at that location but found that it had recently burned down.[15] They continued on. Later that day they encountered two trappers coming downstream in a boat filled with furs. At the foot of Little Rapids, they went ashore to pitch their tent for the first time.

Early the next morning they carried their gear and boat around the first rapid. At the second "Long Rapid," McEntee and Tubby carried the gear around while Puffer pulled the boat upstream through the rapids. Having reached Albany Lake, they paddled to the narrows where they found some rotting timbers, all that remained of the bridge of the old Albany Road. They could still make out the track of the road but it had grown up in trees. A short distance back along that track they found a shanty where they intended to spend the night. The shanty was falling down and smelled foul, so they continued a little farther along the track, where they found a newer shanty and spent the night.

The next two days were spent relaxing, sketching, and fishing on Albany Lake. In the afternoon of the second day another party of four sportsmen from Lowville arrived, led by their guide William Higby.[16]

McEntee immediately liked Higby and imagined him to be the ideal Adirondack guide. Higby showed them how to make tallow candles and also helped them arrange their blankets so they were not so cold at night. They had smoked trout for breakfast the next morning and quickly made the short carry to Smith's Lake. The whole group paddled down Smith's Lake in three boats, wondering at the beauty of the place. Partway down the lake they came to a clearing with a sand beach where Higby had built a camp that spring.

The group stayed at this camp for a week. Their days were spent fishing and exploring. On most days the two artists found time to do a bit of sketching. On one day, McEntee and Tubby climbed Smith's Mountain and explored the remains of David Smith's abandoned cabin. The weather was typical for that time of year with frequent afternoon thunderstorms. On June 24 Puffer, Higby, and the four Lowville men headed back to Lowville. The plan was for Puffer to acquire more provisions and bring the artists their mail.

For the next week the two artists were alone in camp. They did not do well. They were unable to catch any fish on most days. Their experiments with camp cooking were not highly successful. Both of them got sick and found it hard to do anything. They became desperate to see Puffer again. Finally, on the afternoon of July 2, Puffer returned with fresh supplies and some mail and newspapers. On the way back in, Puffer even thought to bring Jimmy O'Kane a new hat and some socks that he told him was a gift from the two artists.

On the morning of July 3, they packed up their camp and headed for their next destination, Brandreth Lake. Their plan was to ascend the largest stream emptying into Smith's Lake. Today that stream is called Shingle Shanty Brook. Puffer apparently had never been up that stream before. After only a short distance, travel became very difficult as the banks closed in. It started to rain. Finally, in desperation, they pulled their boat to shore, picked up their knapsacks, and stumbled through the underbrush following a compass bearing. Just before nightfall they came to the Carthage-to-Lake Champlain Road, where they took shelter in an empty shanty.

*H. Perry Smith (1871)*

Almost exactly twenty years later, in mid-June 1871, H. Perry Smith and seven friends made the same trip as McEntee.[17] Things had not changed much. The group traveled by train from Syracuse and Utica to Martinsburg, the stop before Lowville. At Number Four, Charles Fenton, son of Orrin and Lucy, had built a proper hotel. H. P. Smith's group had a fine dinner there, then continued walking to Stillwater where the Wardwell homestead (see chapter 7) had replaced O'Kane's log cabin. Rather than sleep indoors, they pitched their tent.

The next day they rowed upstream in two collapsible boats they had brought along, each weighing about ninety pounds. They spent that night at Chauncey Smith's log cabin on the South Branch of the Beaver River.[18] The cabin was filled with cast-off gear left behind by former travelers on their way out of the woods. Along one wall were six narrow stalls, each six feet long and wide as a man, with straw ticks on the floor. They spent the next two days at a shanty near the upper end of Albany Lake, then pressed on to Smith's Lake.

Just as they reached Smith's Lake, they were overtaken by a party of eight men they knew from Syracuse, being rowed by five guides. This group was on its way to an improved campsite known as the Syracuse Camp. When they got there, the camp was already occupied. H. P. Smith noted that the Syracuse group "owned the camp by some sort of preemption" and it was always vacated when they arrived.[19] Smith's party continued a bit farther until they found a suitable place to pitch their tents. They explored the lake for two days, fished, and found time to climb Smith's Mountain.

Their next destination was Brandreth Lake. As McEntee had done, they paddled up Shingle Shanty Brook. The banks closed in, causing Smith to remark that the stream "didn't remind us of the Hudson." It rained all day. They camped when they were no longer able to paddle. All the next day they had to carry their gear and boats. As a warning to anyone else who might attempt this traverse, Smith noted, "The streams are obstructed and the carries vague or exist only in the imagination of guides."[20]

There are two other notable features of the H. P. Smith trip. First, one member of the party was a man nicknamed "Ned." Smith remarked tongue-in-cheek that Ned was "one of the most unaccomplished sportsmen among us, and he never improved."[21] Ned was, however, given credit for being a good writer and for having a library of information and maps about the Adirondacks. In fact, "Ned" was Edwin R. Wallace, whose *Descriptive Guide to the Adirondacks* comprises the second half of Smith's book. Wallace's *Guide* proved to be very popular and went on to be published in successive updated editions until 1897.

Second, in 1872 Smith thought that the state should own and preserve all of the land in the region. He specifically argued that the state should not make the Adirondacks more accessible or develop it in any way. "Because, today this vast track, comprising thousands of acres, is one grand natural park, fashioned by the Great Architect of the Universe." In a particularly poetic passage, Smith argued it was important for the state to preserve these lands in their wild conditions. "They should remain so tomorrow and forever; but if we open up this wilderness and avenues through and from it, we but challenge the cupidity of our people; and that which is now magnificent shall become a barren waste."[22] In expressing this sentiment, Smith became one of the earliest advocates of the eventual Adirondack Forest Preserve and Park, which came into being in 1885 and 1892, respectively.

### William W. Hill (1873–78)

As sporting tourism increased, Charles Fenton expanded his hotel by Beaver Lake at Number Four. During July and August 1873, William W. Hill, a prosperous carriage hardware manufacturer from Albany, took up residence at Fenton's with his wife, Jane Woodward Hill, and their three children, one of whom was a thirteen-year-old daughter. Unlike the earlier travelers just described, the Hills made Fenton's their headquarters, taking occasional multiday fishing trips upstream. They visited Stillwater, Smith's Lake, the Red Horse Chain

17. Portrait of William W. Hill, uncredited photograph. Courtesy of the parish archive, St. Paul's Church, Albany, New York.

of Lakes, and other favored fishing holes.[23] Hill was obsessed with fly-fishing for trout and kept meticulous records of his daily catch, which resurfaced in an article he wrote for *Forest and Stream* magazine.[24] The next spring in late May and early June 1874 he made a shorter return fishing trip with three friends, primarily to Smith's Lake.[25]

Hill's outdoors interest changed profoundly when he attended a lecture by Joseph A. Lintner at the Albany Institute on October 20, 1874. At that time the Institute was composed of about two hundred Albany intellectuals drawn from business, law, politics, and science, all of whom either supported or practiced some branch of science. Hill was a new Institute member, only elected earlier in 1874.

Lintner was the head of entomology at the New York State Museum. The title of his talk was "Mr. Otto Meske's Collection of Lepidoptera."[26] Meske was an Albany businessman and amateur butterfly collector working closely with Lintner. As Lintner displayed a few of Meske's cases of mounted beauties, he contrasted the absolute joy of butterfly collecting with dull success in the business world: "What is making money compared to this?"

On that day W. W. Hill found a new and deeply compelling hobby. For the next four summers (1875–78) Hill made extended trips to the Fenton House to collect butterflies.[27] He collected specimens day and night and even enlisted the assistance of fellow guests. Eventually his collection consisted of 2,625 mounted specimens from 42 different species of butterflies and 373 species of moths. It was the first systematic collection of Adirondack butterflies.[28] After W. W. Hill's death, his heirs donated his collection, numbering more than ten thousand specimens, to the New York State Museum, where it comprised a significant part of the museum's collection.[29]

Hill's trips represent the beginning of a new kind of sporting tourism for the Beaver River country. The prime attraction remained fishing and hunting, but the days of sleeping in crude shanties or tents were waning. Beginning at the end of the 1870s, sporting tourists in the Beaver River country would increasingly take their meals and sleep in more comfortable, if simple, backwoods hotels.

# 7

# First Sportsmen's Hotels

## The Creation of the Sportsmen's Hotel

The very first tourists who visited the Beaver River country did not expect to find much in the way of accommodations. Prior to 1870 there was no hotel beyond Orrin and Lucy Fenton's house on the bank of Beaver Lake at Number Four. There were only two known and aforementioned semipermanent shelters farther along the upper Beaver River. At Twitchell Creek stood the old road-builder's cabin occupied from 1845 until 1857 by Jimmy O'Kane. At the sand spring on the South Branch of the Beaver River there was the log cabin built in 1858–59 by Chauncey Smith of Number Four.[1]

In order to camp anywhere else on the upper Beaver River, the guides for sporting tourists would typically build an "open camp." This consisted of a lean-to made of saplings and roofed with bark stripped from a nearby tree. Fresh evergreen boughs were used inside the open camp to provide some protection from the hard, cold ground. A carefully constructed open camp could last for two or three years before needing to be rebuilt.[2] Such semipermanent structures soon dotted the upper Beaver River at the outlet of the Red Horse Creek and along the shores of Albany and Smith's lakes. Some early campers also carried canvas tents that could be used if no other convenient shelter was at hand.[3]

About 1870 the first sportsmen's lodging beyond Fenton's opened at the William Wardwell homestead on the west side of the bridge over Twitchell Creek at Stillwater. By the time Wardwell bought this property, the cabin O'Kane formerly occupied at that spot had long

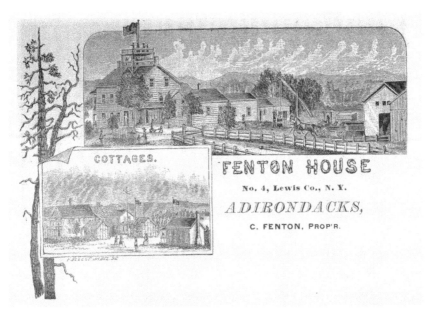

18. The Fenton House, uncredited wood engraving. Wallace, *Guide*, p. 97.

since crumbled into mold. Located at a prime jumping-off spot for
the upper Beaver River along the Carthage-to-Lake Champlain Road,
Wardwell's soon became popular with sporting tourists.

Three new sportsmen's hotels opened on the upper Beaver River
at the end of the 1870s. The Wardwells sold out to the Dunbar family
in 1878. The Dunbars built a proper frame hotel building and later
added cabins, a boathouse, and docks. Maps from after 1878 changed
the designation of the land at Twitchell Creek from Wardwell's to
Dunbar's.[4] About the same time that Dunbar's came into existence,
two new hotels opened farther upstream. At Little Rapids a modest
place called Muncy's[5] opened in 1878. About the same time a former
guide's camp at Smith's Lake was converted into a sportsmen's hotel
called Smith's Lake Hotel. Originally built by a guide named S. Boyd
Edwards, this hotel was later operated by the Lamont family.[6]

The four hotels were similar in many ways, although each had its
own special features and outbuildings. All of them had a two-story
rectangular frame main hotel building, two to three times as long as it

was wide, sometimes with only a half story under the roof. The family lived in a few core rooms downstairs around the kitchen. Guests slept upstairs. Privacy was limited. Rooms were sometimes not plastered and might have blankets for doors. At Lamont's there was also a separate building that resembled a logger's bunkhouse, with multiple cots in one room.

Another way that the sportsmen's hotels of the time were similar is the fact that women managed them. Even though guidebooks and other published accounts of the time referred to the hotels using only the husband's name, the hotels could not have existed without these women. While their husbands worked in the woods as guides or loggers, it was the women who ran the hotel business. With the help of their children they cooked simple meals, raised their own perishable food, and kept small livestock to supplement the fish and game their guests expected. Women did the bookkeeping and kept the bedrooms furnished with clean blankets and reasonably comfortable mattresses.[7]

Of the five early sportsmen's hotels in the Beaver River country, we know women managed four of them.[8] At Number Four, Lucy Weller Fenton managed the Fenton House from 1826 until 1863. At Stillwater, Sarah C. Wardwell managed Wardwell's from 1870 until 1878 with the help of her daughter Rosa. Mary E. Warmwood Dunbar managed the Dunbar Hotel from 1878 until 1892 with the assistance of her four children and two nephews. At Smith's Lake, Ella Gordon Lamont managed Lamont's Hotel with the help of her two children from about 1886 until 1891.

## The Early Sportsmen's Hotels

### *Fenton House at Number Four*

As mentioned in chapter 3, Orrin Fenton was one of the early settlers of Number Four, having arrived in 1826. As was the case with most nineteenth-century sportsmen's hotels, the Fenton family got into the hotel business by renting rooms in the homestead to the occasional passersby. As the number of visitors increased, they periodically

19. Fenton House, uncredited photo postcard. Courtesy of Frank Carey.

enlarged their accommodations. By 1851 Fenton's had a reputation
among sportsmen for decent lodgings and good food.[9]

Fenton's remained a modest place during the rest of Orrin Fenton's tenure. He and his second wife, Lucy Weller Fenton, raised their
five children at Number Four while eking out a wilderness subsistence
by renting rooms, guiding, hunting, fishing, and gardening.[10] After
residing in the woods for nearly forty years, in 1863 the Fentons reluc-
tantly sold their hotel to Losee B. Lewis and moved to the village of
Watson.[11] Orrin Fenton was something of a North Country legend by
the time he finally moved to town. W. Hudson Stephens, the Lowville
attorney who presided at the closing of the sale of the original Fenton
House, mused:

> The silence and solitude of the northern forest has had its charms
> for him. Who will say his heart's earlier aspirations have not been
> as effectively satisfied in the solitude of the uncultivated forest, as

20. Fenton House sitting room, Number Four, New York, uncredited photo postcard. Courtesy of Frank Carey.

if he had moved amid the crowded haunts of the busy city? This
sportsman by land and stream, this forest farmer, looks back upon
the woodland scene and experience with sighs.[12]

Presumably Lewis continued to operate a sportsmen's hotel at
Number Four until 1870, when Orrin and Lucy Fenton's son, Charles,
returned and repurchased the original Fenton House. Orrin having just
died, Charles may have used his share of the inheritance to build a new
three-story hotel at Number Four at the cost of five thousand dollars.
Wallace's first guidebook highly recommended the enlarged Fenton
House. It could accommodate up to fifty guests by 1872. Ten years later,
with the addition of cabins and extensions on the main building, it could
accommodate one hundred.[13] For the rest of the nineteenth century,
Fenton's was regarded as a comfortable wilderness resort, as well as the
first stop for parties traveling farther into the Beaver River country.[14]

When Charles Fenton retired around the turn of the twentieth century, he turned running the hotel over to his daughter, Cora

Fenton Parker. She operated the Fenton House until 1941, when she sold it to Henrietta Lowe Patterson of Dayton, Ohio. Mrs. Patterson entrusted the operation of the hotel to locals George Oaster and William Becker. Within a few years these two men formed a partnership and bought the Fenton property. Oaster later drowned at Stillwater during a storm, and Becker bought out his share. Becker sold the hotel to Vincent Ross in 1952. Much of the complex burned in 1965, causing Ross to close the hotel. Another fire in 1981 destroyed the rest of the buildings except for a few of the cottages.[15]

### Wardwell's at Stillwater

The *Lowville Journal and Republican* for May 18, 1870, contains the first reference to the existence of a sportsmen's hotel at Stillwater. Although that article refers to the "Tuttle Hotel," a name derived from a nearby glacial pothole called Tuttle Pond, the lodging in question was the homestead of the family of William Wardwell.

William Wardwell was born about 1830 in Martinsburg in the Black River Valley south of Lowville. He married Sarah C. (maiden name unknown) in 1855, and in 1858 their daughter Rosa was born. He worked as a house painter before being drafted in 1864 to fight in the Civil War. He served one year, then returned to his family.[16]

The steadily growing number of sporting tourists visiting the upper Beaver River must have been the reason the Wardwells decided they could make a better living by homesteading and accommodating visitors at a wilderness outpost at Stillwater. They bought fifty acres on the west side of Twitchell Creek at the confluence with the Beaver River near the Twitchell Creek Road bridge.[17] They built a basic log house, a barn, and some outbuildings on the bluff overlooking a deep pool about a quarter of a mile back from the main river. They called this homestead "The Wild Woods Home."[18]

In no time, local outdoors guides started storing boats and supplies at Wardwell's. There was a pasture for horses and a place where wagons could be stored. The two guides hired by the H. Perry Smith party used it this way in the summer of 1871. Wardwell's cabin was apparently too small for a party of eight and their guides, so they also pitched a tent.[19]

Wardwell was a friendly but eccentric character. He claimed to be a crack shot, but visitor A. Judd Northrup noted the gunsight on his rifle was only loosely tied on with a leather thong. The roof of his log barn had tumbled in, but Wardwell laconically told Northrup he would repair it "when I git ta it."[20] W. W. Hill and his wife visited on a fishing trip 1873. They found that Wardwell's was "in very comfortable shape for a place so far back in the forest, and is kept neat and tidy by Mrs. W. and her daughter, Rosa."[21] Fifteen-year-old Rosa especially impressed the Hills because she "can fish and row a boat as well as she can talk."

Charles Fenton stopped at Wardwell's on March 10, 1875, on a trip to Albany Lake guiding two sportsmen from Massachusetts who wanted to go ice fishing for lake trout. They picked up a small stove at Wardwell's that Fenton had stored there to use for winter camping. Wardwell, his wife, and his seventy-year-old mother were happy for company as they had not left home since the first of January. On the way back to Number Four, Fenton met Wardwell and his daughter Rosa on the road. They were walking home on snowshoes from Lowville where Rosa had been attending school. According to Fenton, Rosa covered the eleven miles from Number Four to Stillwater in just three and a half hours without feeling tired.[22]

Between 1870 and 1876 the Wardwells played host to almost every passing party visiting the upper Beaver River. Wardwell's provided travelers with a simple meal of trout or venison and a place to sleep out of the rain. The Wardwell homestead was not a destination, but a welcome waystation. The spot near Twitchell Creek at Stillwater was soon being shown on maps as "Wardwell's."[23]

Sometime in 1875 or 1876 Sarah Wardwell fell seriously ill and was confined to bed.[24] The *Lowville Journal and Republican* for April 5, 1876, reported that the Wardwells had moved back to town and hired Edmund Burdick and his wife to run the hotel for the summer season. A sporting party that passed that way in the fall of 1876 noted that a guide named Henry Burke had taken over the host's duties at

Stillwater.[25] Wardwell's was last mentioned in Wallace's *Descriptive Guide to the Adirondacks* in the 1876 edition.

By the summer of 1877, Joseph Dunbar was in residence at Wardwell's. He had arranged to purchase the place and even convinced Frank Tweedy of the Colvin surveying party working in the area to mark out the boundary. Presumably, Sarah Wardwell eventually recovered from the illness that forced the family to leave their Stillwater homestead. After the untimely death of Rosa in 1882, William and Sarah moved west to Wisconsin.

### The Dunbar Hotel at Stillwater

When Joe Dunbar and his family moved to Stillwater in 1877, Adirondack sporting tourism was growing fast. There were already over two hundred hotels and inns of various styles and sizes operating all across the Adirondacks. Even far back in the forest at Stillwater there was a slowly growing need for better and larger accommodations.

The Dunbar family replaced Wardwell's cabin with a simple but substantial two-story frame hotel and half a dozen cabins. This hotel soon became a destination for adventurous visitors who wanted a slightly more refined taste of the wilderness. Soon the location along the west shore of Twitchell Creek at the junction with the Beaver River came to be known as "Dunbar's meadow" or just "Dunbar's."[26]

Joseph C. Dunbar was born in 1839 in Sodus, Wayne County, New York. When he was still a child, his family moved to the western edge of the forest at

21. Cabins of the Dunbar Hotel about 1890, uncredited photograph from the Churchill-Shaver Album. Courtesy of Jim and Carol Fox.

Greig in Lewis County. He married Mary E. Warmwood of Greig in 1862. They moved two miles north of Dannatberg, cleared wilderness land, and built a farm. Joe was later employed as a foreman for Lewis, Crawford & Company at Chase's Lake; the firm made hemlock bark extract for tanning.[27] Between 1863 and 1873, Joe and Mary had four children: Lucy, James, Albert, and Talcott.

The Dunbar family obtained legal title to Wardwell's in 1877 or 1878.[28] Dunbar's soon became a popular alternate to Fenton's, especially with sportsmen who wanted to stay in the upper part of the Beaver River. Published accounts praised the hotel. Raymond Hopper remarked in *Forest and Stream*, "Dunbar's, the only house at Stillwater, is well kept and a favorite place to many; there we got our first venison steak and a comfortable lodging."[29] William Morris noted, "Jolly Joe Dunbar, the proprietor of the hotel there, will receive you in hearty backwoods style. Joe will give you supper, lodging and breakfast of good quality for one dollar and fifty cents each."[30]

Over the next fifteen years, Joe Dunbar became widely known as a good host and an unsurpassed guide. The hotel was expanded periodically and became a favorite of modestly wealthy sportsmen from across Central New York. Dunbar's had enough business to keep at least half a dozen other guides busy during the hunting and fishing seasons.[31]

Joe Dunbar looked like everybody's idea of an Adirondack guide. For hunting, he wore homemade buckskin moccasins with the hair on. He was said to be one of the toughest men in the state and could endure great hardships. Supposedly he was able to sleep out of doors in the snow with the thermometer below zero.[32] Like many guides of that era, Dunbar did not believe the game laws applied to him. This resulted in his arrest, along with his son Talcott, for illegal deer hunting in December 1888.[33]

The entire Dunbar family, including the teenage children, was involved in operating the hotel. The Dunbars also employed two young nephews, William and Chester Elliott. Both these young men stayed in the hotel business: William became the proprietor of the Central Hotel in Lowville, while Chet became a guide and later

22. "Joe" Dunbar, uncredited photograph. *Eighth and Ninth Reports of the Forest, Fish and Game Commission 1902–1903*, facing p. 284.

opened his own sportsmen's hotel near Beaver River Station. James "Jim" Dunbar followed in his father's footsteps and also became a guide.[34]

A curious addition to the family occurred about 1882 when Joe and Mary Dunbar adopted an infant daughter who they named Rose. No information is available about Rose's parents. It seems plausible that Rose was the child of Lucy Dunbar, who would have been nineteen at the time of Rose's birth.

In December 1892, the founders of the Beaver River Club purchased Dunbar's Hotel.[35] The Dunbar family returned to their farm in Greig, except for Jim who stayed on to work as the dam-keeper and a guide. A year later Joe, Mary, and their adopted child Rose moved to a farm on the outskirts of Batavia, Genesee Country, New York. Joseph Dunbar died on April 16, 1910, at the age of seventy-one. Mary Dunbar died two years later, in September 1913.

### Muncy's at Little Rapids

By 1877, Andrew J. Muncy had built a simple wilderness hotel at Little Rapids, where he leased about fifty acres.[36] His rectangular building measured fifty-two feet by thirty-six feet.

Muncy's was about a five-hour row in a guideboat from Dunbar's at Stillwater.[37] Because it was right on the carry trail to Albany Lake,

23. Muncy's Hotel at Little Rapids in 1887, cabinet card by F. E. Slocum of Lowville, New York. Courtesy of Michael Hess.

visitors who left Dunbar's in the morning often stopped there for dinner, their midday meal. Muncy's could also be reached by a spur off the Carthage-to-Lake Champlain Road. Muncy maintained the road as far as his place because he needed to use his horses and wagon to bring in supplies from Lowville.[38]

### Lamont's Smith's Lake Hotel

As more and more sportsmen visited Smith's Lake during the 1870s, Beaver River guides developed well-appointed camps consisting of multiple shanties for sleeping, dining shelters with rustic furniture, and other small buildings where heavier gear could be stored during the season. The camps were situated at various scenic spots along the lake shore near freshwater springs. They could be used by anyone so long as no damage was done and with the understanding that should the guide who built the camp show up, any other occupants would move elsewhere. For example, when H. Perry Smith and his party stopped at the Syracuse Camp during their visit in 1871, they saw the eight members of the Syracuse party "sweeping up the outlet" and politely vacated the camp.[39] Wallace's *Guide* for 1875 and 1878 specifically mentions the Syracuse camp, and notes there were also other fine open camps available all around the lake.

By 1878 S. Boyd Edwards, one of the guides who helped build and maintain the Syracuse camp, had erected a two-story log bunkhouse on the west side of the lake near the Syracuse camp. He called it the Smith's Lake Hotel.[40] Sometime after 1878 but before 1886, this camp was acquired by the James Lamont family.[41] The compound eventually included a cabin for the family, additional sleeping quarters, an indoor kitchen, and several guest cabins in addition to the original two-story log dormitory. It could accommodate forty people "in an always

24. Lamont's Hotel on Smith's Lake (Lake Lila), uncredited photograph. *Eighth and Ninth Reports of the Forest, Fish and Game Commission, 1902–1903*, facing p. 292.

comfortable but decidedly backwoods style."[42] Travelers described this rustic hotel as comfortable and beautifully situated.[43] By 1891, even though far back in the forest, Lamont's had a rare telephone connection to the outside world.[44]

James Lamont was born in Diana in Lewis County around 1850. He married Ella Gordon, also a Lewis County native, in March 1872. They had a son, Carroll, and a daughter, Nina, before they became hotelkeepers at Smith's Lake. Ella Lamont was described as "an educated and superior woman, and [who] with two grown children, assists materially in making the backwoods lodging comfortable and interesting." James Lamont was affectionately referred to as "Uncle Jim," as was common for Adirondack guides of the time.[45] In an interesting twist, Ella Lamont was apparently universally known as "Auntie Jim."[46]

Sportsman Raymond Hopper greatly admired James Lamont. Hopper noted, "Although not a powerful man in appearance, yet

James Lamont is as muscular and wiry as anyone I have ever known of his build; in fact, he has the reputation of being able to cover more territory in the woods in less time than anyone of the guides no matter what the general conditions may be."

By January 1891, Lowville businessman William Morrison had purchased the land around Smith's Lake and part of Albany Lake.[47] His plan was to start a sportsmen's club called the Smith's Lake Park Association. The purchase included Lamont's Hotel. Morrison erected a new two-story building especially to house the ladies. The Lamonts were hired to operate the new club.

It was not to be. In June 1891, Dr. William Seward Webb, about whom we will learn much more in chapters 8 and 9, purchased all the land around the headwaters of the Beaver River, including Lamont's and all of Morrison's land.[48] Webb posted the lands from Little Rapids to Smith's Lake against trespass and closed Lamont's and Muncy's to the public.[49] About a year later, in December 1892, the Beaver River Club closed Dunbar's Hotel to the public and posted no trespassing signs on the 6,250 surrounding acres.

Thus, the era of the early sporting tourist ended, as almost all the land surrounding the upper Beaver River passed into the hands of owners determined to prevent public access. As will be seen in the next part of this book, the plan to make the upper Beaver River an exclusive private reserve did not survive for long. During the next few years, a series of events that could not have been predicted resulted in much of the land around the upper Beaver River becoming the property of the state and being reopened to the public.

# Part Three

# Dams, Railroad, and Beaver River Station

25. Beaver River Dam, Herkimer County, New York, showing construction of the gatehouse and inlet of tunnel in progress, July 15, 1903, uncredited photograph. *Annual Report of the State Engineer and Surveyor of the State of New York for the Fiscal Year Ending September 30, 1903,* facing p. 226.

26. NYC Station, Beaver River, New York, uncredited photo postcard. Courtesy of Frank Carey.

# 8

# Creation of the
# Stillwater Reservoir

The Stillwater Reservoir is the most prominent physical feature of
the Beaver River country, other than the forest. Stretching for eleven
miles, and a mile wide at places, it is one of the largest and most remote
bodies of water in the Adirondacks. This chapter describes why the
reservoir was created and how it profoundly altered the Beaver River
country.[1]

## Possible Log-Driving Dams: 1850–85

The earliest dams on the Beaver River were probably log-driving dams
intended to collect adequate water so logs could be floated downstream
to market. There is no conclusive evidence indicating when dams of
this type were first built on the Beaver River. We do know that Lyman
Rasselas Lyon bought most of the forest surrounding the west end
of the present-day Stillwater Reservoir from the descendants of John
Brown in 1850.[2] Lyon immediately started commercial logging in the
Beaver River area, so it is probably safe to assume temporary logging
dams were first built about at that time.

Logging along the Beaver River was widespread enough that in
1853 the state legislature declared the Beaver River a "public highway" for floating logs to market.[3] Logging interests generally sought
this designation so they had the legal right to build temporary dams
and modify stream banks by removing snags, overhanging trees, rock
obstructions, and such.

27. Photograph of a dam for making freshet for floating logs in Northern Michigan, uncredited photograph. US National Archives and Records Administration, image NARA 2129578.

Log-driving dams were relatively inexpensive to build since they were constructed out of local timber and earth. They sometimes lasted for several years with modest annual repairs, and could be entirely replaced when needed. A typical feature of these dams was a floodgate that could be opened to allow a rush of water filled with logs to cascade downstream. The most common term given to this type of temporary log-driving dam is "splash dam" or "flood dam."[4]

In 1864, the New York legislature appropriated ten thousand dollars to improve the channel of the Beaver River for the purpose of floating logs.[5] The channel was altered in places from the mouth of Sunday Creek, about six miles below Stillwater, all the way upstream to the headwaters at Smith's Lake. A channel sixteen to twenty feet wide was blasted out of the rock from Stillwater to Sunday Creek. Upstream above Stillwater an oxbow was cut through at a spot called Dutch Gap. A low logging dam was built at the outlet of Smith's Lake.[6] By 1865 the Beaver River was judged suitable for floating thirteen-foot softwood logs all the way from Smith's Lake to the Black River.

There is no evidence that a logging dam was built prior to 1885 in the section of the river that would eventually become the reservoir. Verplanck Colvin visited the Beaver River country on several occasions during his monumental Adirondack survey (1872–1900). During the summer of 1878, a Colvin survey team created the first accurate map of the upper Beaver River from Albany Lake to Beaver Lake.[7] This map of the great marsh of the Beaver River above Stillwater shows no flooded land or other evidence of a dam anywhere in that part of the river.

## The First Wood and Earth Dam: 1885–87

The Black River Canal was completed in 1850. As soon as it opened, commercial interests all along the Black River complained that the canal was diverting so much water from the river that they did not have adequate water power to operate on a regular schedule year-round. As early as 1851, the state legislature passed a bill authorizing a survey to determine suitable locations for reservoirs to supply the Black River Canal and to replace water in the Black River diverted to the Erie Canal.[8] The survey concluded that the branches of the Moose and upper Black Rivers, watersheds south of the Beaver, provided the best locations for water supply reservoirs. Between 1851 and 1880, the state erected a series of reservoirs on the Moose and upper Black Rivers.[9]

Unfortunately, the early Moose and Black River reservoirs proved inadequate to keep both the Black River and the canal at acceptable levels. In 1881, the legislature authorized dams on the Beaver and Independence Rivers as well as six new dams on the Moose and Black Rivers, including two new dams on the Fulton Chain.[10] After preliminary scouting, James Galvin,[11] superintendent, section 2 of Black River Canal, and James Shanahan, superintendent of public works, decided the first Beaver River dam should be built at Stillwater above the rapids. Following this decision, plans for a dam on the Independence River were abandoned.

28. The 1887 Stillwater dam, uncredited photograph from the Churchill-Shaver Album. Courtesy of Jim and Carol Fox.

The first state impoundment dam at Stillwater was built at a narrow section of the river a short distance downstream from the junction with Twitchell Creek. It was a simple timber and earth dam that rose nine and a half feet above natural low water with a long spillway to allow logs to be driven over the dam. It impounded about 328 million cubic feet of water at capacity.

Work on the dam began in July 1885 but soon stopped when someone noticed that the law authorizing the dam required it to be built in Lewis County, whereas the site was in Herkimer County. The legislature refused to disburse payments for work done in the wrong county. During the next legislative session, the law was amended to allow the dam to be built in Herkimer County. Work on the dam resumed in July 1886 and was completed in early 1887.

The first dam submerged portions of the Beaver River marsh up to the edge of the forest for about five miles upstream. A shallow lake developed near the confluence of the Beaver River with Twitchell Creek, and the river upstream became wider about to the place where the Red Horse Creek flowed in. This first impoundment was called the Beaver River Flow.

Although the first dam was designed not to interfere with log driving, the higher water did flood a significant amount of forest that could have been logged. On September 26, 1888, Mary Lyon Fisher, heir of Lyman R. Lyon who then owned 9,500 acres of forest lands in the area, brought suit against New York State because of a disagreement about how much of her land at the junction of the Beaver River and Twitchell Creek had been rendered unusable. New York State eventually settled with Fisher by purchasing 1,594.22 acres for the sum of $9,970.[12]

## The Second Wood and Earth Dam: 1893–94

It was soon obvious that the first Stillwater dam did not impound nearly enough water for the waterpower needs of the Black River. In fact, some legislators in Albany accused the superintendent of public works, who designed and sited the Stillwater dam, of catering to the interests of lumbermen over the interests of Black River businesses.

Finally, in 1892, the legislature authorized funds to enlarge and improve the Beaver River dam at Stillwater.[13] The new dam was to have a total height of fourteen and a half feet, five feet higher than the first dam. Construction began in 1893 and was completed by early 1894. The new dam was probably built at the same location as the first dam, most likely right on top of the 1887 dam. The 1894 dam created a larger Beaver River Flow that extended 9.3 miles upstream and had a surface area of 2,688 acres. Because the trees in the flooded area were not cut down, the Flow became an uninviting piece of water studded with rotting dead trees.[14]

The most significant outcome of the 1894 dam's construction was that it made log driving from above the dam impossible.[15] Dr. William Seward Webb, who had recently purchased a huge tract of virgin timber upstream from the dam and planned large-scale logging operations, sued New York State for $184,350.60 in damages resulting from

29. The 1894 State dam on the Beaver River, photo by J. F. Severance, *Second Annual Report of the Commissioners of Fisheries, Game and Forests*, facing p. 460.

the loss of value of the timber on 65,836 acres that he claimed now could not be lumbered.[16]

Faced with this lawsuit as well as claims for damages from downstream industries that suffered from inadequate water supply, the state entered into negotiations with Dr. Webb. The legislature authorized the Fisheries, Game and Forest Commission,[17] upon approval by the commissioners of the Land Office, to purchase tracts of lands, not exceeding eighty thousand acres, where owners sustained damages resulting from construction of dams for canal purposes or to restore waters taken for canal purposes.[18] Shortly after this bill became law, Dr. Webb advised the commissioners that he was prepared to settle the matter by selling the state outright approximately seventy-five thousand acres of his forest for the sum of six hundred thousand dollars. This was more than three times the amount Webb originally claimed as damages, but, of course, the state would end up with title to the land.

In support of the asking price, Webb presented expert testimony to the investigating committee appointed by the commissioners.

Forty-two witnesses, including lumbermen, local guides, hotel own-ers, prominent sportsmen, and even medical doctors, testified over the course of a week. The transcript of this testimony runs to 1,547 pages. During the month of July 1895, a party of state officials includ-ing the Fisheries, Game and Forest commissioners and representa-tives of the Land Board made a tour of the Beaver River country to inspect the affected lands. They hunted, fished, and dined at Webb's Nehasane Park, inspected the dam, dined at the Forge House, and even stopped to say hello to ex-president Benjamin Harrison at his retreat at Second Lake.[19]

Webb's offer was then discussed and approved by the investigat-ing committee in a meeting in Albany held on December 6, 1895. The sale was approved by the full Commission and Land Board on December 31, 1895, and the purchase closed on January 16, 1896.[20] The purchase agreement was extensive[21] and contained important spe-cial exceptions.[22]

The Webb purchase was the first addition to the Adirondack For-est Preserve in the Beaver River country. It was the largest single pur-chase by the state for the Forest Preserve and remained so until recent times. In fact, most of the Forest Preserve land in the Beaver River country was acquired in the Webb purchase.[23]

### Forest Preserve and Park

Simultaneously with the construction of the early Stillwater dams, the decade of 1885–94 saw three steps that forever altered how the Adiron-dacks and the Beaver River country were managed: the creation of the Adirondack Forest Preserve in 1885, creation of the Adirondack Park in 1892, and passage of the "Forever Wild" amendment to the state constitution in 1894. The purpose of the Forest Preserve law[24] was to set aside and manage all the state-owned forest in the Adirondacks and the Catskills in order to assure a future supply of clean water for the state's cities and canals. The law provided that Forest Preserve lands shall be kept "forever wild" and that they could not be "sold, leased or taken by any person or corporation, public or private."[25]

Although the state's Adirondack lands were technically protected from the worst tactics of the lumber industry, the Forest Commission appointed under the 1885 law was closely allied to lumbering interests. In fact, a lumberman from the Beaver River area, Theodore Basselin, was appointed one of the commissioners. While sale of Forest Preserve *land* was prohibited, the law did not specify that its *timber* could not be sold. Over the next eight years the Forest Commission routinely approved applications from lumbermen to harvest timber on the Forest Preserve. In 1893, the legislature retroactively approved many of these practices by giving the commission the right to sell timber from Forest Preserve lands and trade Forest Preserve land for other land as it saw fit.[26]

Those who saw the Forest Preserve as the way to save the Adirondacks from the depredations of the lumber barons felt betrayed, especially after they had advocated for the 1892 creation of the Adirondack Park, which incorporated the Forest Preserve and was intended to give it an extra layer of protection. Opposition to the 1893 "cutting law" grew in many quarters, including sportsmen's clubs, some professional foresters, and the all-important New York City business associations, who understood that preservation of the forest meant preservation of a steady supply of water to the state's canals, on which they relied for their commerce.[27]

When New York State held a constitutional convention in 1894, the politically powerful New York Board of Trade and Transportation saw an opportunity to remedy the situation. At their prompting, a constitutional amendment was introduced that was designed to put the Forest Preserve out of reach of the lumbermen once and for all. A delegate-at-large from Syracuse, William P. Goodelle, proposed adding the word "destroyed" to the end of section 7 of the proposed amendment, a move specifically intended to prevent Forest Preserve land from being used to build reservoirs. The entire constitutional amendment was later approved unanimously.

Goodelle was a founding member of the Beaver River Club (see chapter 11). Based on his personal experience, he believed that the Forest Commission was systematically manipulating the water released from the Stillwater dam to benefit the downstream logging business of Theodore Basselin, one of the three commissioners. Goodelle was also appalled at the number of trees standing dead in the water behind the 1894 dam.[28] He thought prohibiting the destruction of trees on the Forest Preserve was a certain way to prevent future reservoirs from being built in the Adirondacks.[29]

Article 7, section 7 of the constitution, popularly known as the "Forever Wild" amendment, went into effect on January 1, 1895. It provided that "the lands of the state, now owned or hereafter acquired, constituting the forest preserve as now fixed by law, shall be forever kept as wild forest lands. They shall not be leased, sold, or exchanged, or be taken by any corporation, public or private, nor shall the timber thereon be sold, removed, or destroyed." Although those who favored conservation believed that this constitutional provision permanently protected the Forest Preserve, in the matter of reservoirs, the battle was not over.

## The First Concrete Dam: 1902–3

Although the 1894 dam served its intended purposes fairly well, like all wood and earth dams it leaked and required frequent repairs. Accordingly, in 1900 the legislature authorized a more substantial replacement dam to be built "as near as possible to the current dam."[30] The spillway of the new dam was to be made of concrete. The capacity of the new dam was greater even though the overall effective depth remained unchanged because about 105 additional acres would be flooded between the site of the new dam and the old dam.[31] The rationale for the new dam was the same as before, to assure adequate waterpower to businesses located on the Black River. As an indication of how important reliable water flow was to downstream manufacturers, the Black River Power Owners Association raised ten thousand dollars by subscription to buy the land that would be flooded by the new dam.[32]

Construction started in January 1902. Construction equipment was brought by train to Beaver River Station, then hauled to the site by horses. The new dam, built at the brink of the uppermost falls,

30. The 1902 state dam, Beaver River, New York, uncredited photo postcard. Courtesy of Frank Carey.

consisted of two separate parts. On the north side, an earth dam was built across the natural channel of the river. The dirt dam had a concrete core twelve feet thick at the base tapering to four feet wide at the top. The dirt side of the dam butted up to an existing granite block one hundred feet wide on the south.

The second part of the dam, termed the spillway dam, was built on the south side of the granite block. This was a curved all-concrete dam with an effective depth of twelve feet. The top was five feet wide and the base from twelve to twenty-five feet wide depending on the terrain. A rectangular gatehouse was built at the top of the spillway dam on the south bank.

This was a massive construction project employing more than one hundred workers. Before work could begin, housing needed to be built near the site, as well as warehouses for material, a saw and planing mill, a blacksmith shop, and office buildings. A 3,600-foot-long tramway was constructed from the existing 1894 wooden dam to the construction site to allow heavy materials to be delivered by water from

Beaver River Station. A 900-foot-long tunnel was blasted out of solid rock at the base of the dam to be used as a floodgate. An artificial river channel twenty-five feet wide was dug to divert the course of the river into the tunnel while the dam was under construction.

The construction suffered a number of setbacks. It had been a snowy winter. Workers had to clear four feet of snow from the area between the 1894 dam and the new location a bit farther downstream before the necessary buildings could be constructed. When all that snow melted in the spring, the greater than usual runoff overtopped the 1894 wood dam and flooded part of the construction site. If that was not enough, when the state engineers inspected the concrete delivered to the site, they found 1,300 of the 1,500 barrels did not meet specifications and had to be replaced.

Finally, in the spring of 1903 the gates closed on the new dam and the water began to rise. The 1894 dam was not removed and its remains can still be seen at times of very low water.[33]

## The Current Concrete Dam: 1922–25

As previously noted, the water power requirements of Black River manufacturers caused by diversion of water to the Erie Canal by the Black River Canal was the impetus for the initial dam-building at Stillwater.[34] By the turn of the twentieth century, however, use of the Black River Canal had declined to the point that it ceased operations north of Boonville. Some segments of the canal remained in use until about 1920, but in 1925 the Black River Canal was officially declared abandoned.

Nonetheless, industries all along the course of the Black River, especially in Watertown, ran on waterpower, and the existing reservoirs were still not supplying enough. As the demand for waterpower increased throughout northern New York, talk began in Albany about enlarging a number of existing dams and building new dams in various locations throughout the Adirondacks. In addition, some industries had switched to electric power and hydroelectric power was a tantalizing prospect.[35] Opponents of dam-building in the Adirondack Park pointed out that the land surrounding the proposed dams was part of the Adirondack Forest Preserve. As noted, the state constitution forbade sale or destruction of any of those lands. The resulting political struggle was termed "the Black River War."[36]

The political might of those in favor of new and bigger dams was formidable. To circumvent the constitutional restrictions on alienating land or destroying the timber of the Forest Preserve, in 1913 the legislature passed the Burd Amendment to the Forest Preserve Act. It specifically allowed for up to three percent of the Forest Preserve's six million acres to be flooded to create or enlarge reservoirs.

The powerful New York Board of Trade and Transportation opposed building any new dams on the Forest Preserve. They lobbied the governor and the legislature to create a statewide plan to increase water storage and waterpower. Long a champion of the Forest Preserve, they argued for enlarging the Forest Preserve and further limiting logging to protect water resources.[37]

Nonetheless, in 1915 the legislature passed the Machold Storage Law, which provided for the creation of river regulating districts, subject to approval by the Conservation Commission. Once approved, a regulating district was empowered to build dams, construct reservoirs, and alter or regulate river flow. The next year the Conservation Commission made a study of the waterpower needs of the Black River. The report discussed various dam-building possibilities on the Beaver River and concluded that before building a dam at Lake Lila or Beaver Lake the regulating district should consider impounding all the needed water in an enlarged Stillwater Reservoir.[38]

Pursuant to the Machold Storage Law, the Black River Regulating District was created in 1919.[39] This agency assumed control of the dams on the Moose, Black, and Beaver Rivers, including the dam at Stillwater. In 1920, the Black River Regulating District received preliminary approval of a plan to construct twelve dams and accompanying reservoirs on Forest Preserve land. The Regulating District swiftly evaluated the feasibility of building these dams. The Moose River dams at Old Forge and Sixth Lake were not considered suitable for enlargement because popular resort areas were already growing up around them. The Regulating District decided the three most feasible projects would be to enlarge the Stillwater dam and build two dams on the Moose River, one near Panther Mountain and one near Higley Mountain.[40] In 1920 the Black River Regulating District received final approval from the Conservation Commission to raise the Stillwater dam by nineteen feet to its current height of thirty-three and a half feet.

Owners of the private land that would be flooded were aware that the state planned to enlarge the dam as early as 1919, if not earlier. The Black River Regulating District drew detailed maps of the area to be flooded by the larger reservoir.[41] The regulating district, acting as purchasing agent for the state, then negotiated purchases of all the land below the projected future high-water line. The regulating district was not interested in purchasing buildings, only the land.[42]

Many of the owners of property in the area to be flooded had built substantial camps. The state gave them until the end of 1924 to remove their buildings or have them destroyed. As the state systematically acquired this land during the early 1920s, quite a few camps were moved to higher ground using teams of draft horses and rollers. A number of these relocated camps still exist in the vicinity of Beaver River Station and Stillwater.[43]

The Regulating District held a public hearing at the end of August 1921 to take comments on the planned dam expansion.[44] The town of Webb and the owners of Fisher Forestry Company complained that the road would be flooded. The New York Central Railroad complained that a long section of track would need to be relocated. Representatives of the regulating district dismissed these complaints as of little consequence. An attorney appearing on behalf of six members of the Beaver River Club argued that the flooding of his client's valuable property was unconstitutional.[45] He noted that the proposed enlargement of the dam violated the state constitution's prohibition of destruction of Forest Preserve land and timber because about four thousand acres of Forest Preserve would be flooded. If the dam expansion were unconstitutional, then exercise of eminent domain by the Regulating District under the Storage Law would also be unconstitutional.

The constitutional question clearly worried the regulating district. The question of whether the legislature had overstepped its constitutional authority when it passed the 1915 Machold Storage Law had never been determined by the courts. This constitutional issue temporarily stood in the way of expanding the reservoir.

One of the owners of a lot on the Beaver River Club was Wilson D. Ogsbury, a real estate investor from Watertown, New York.[46] When the Black River Regulating District tried to use eminent domain to force him to sell his lot in 1922, he refused, claiming the dam expansion was unconstitutional. In response the regulating district filed suit against Ogsbury.[47] At trial Ogsbury submitted virtually no evidence, causing the judge to wonder whether the regulating district may have orchestrated the whole proceeding for the sole purpose of obtaining a precedent-setting decision. As soon as the New York Court of Appeals issued a final decision finding the use of eminent domain by the regulating district was constitutional, Ogsbury sold his lot.[48] The other remaining members of the Beaver River Club did the same.

While the Ogsbury case was still in litigation, logging crews began to clear the approximately four thousand acres that would be flooded by the enlarged dam. The 1924 dam was built on the same foundation as the 1902 dam. The concrete spillway dam was enlarged and the earth dam was increased in height. The gatehouse of the 1902 dam was raised to the top of the new dam. On February 11, 1925, the gates closed at the new Stillwater dam and the water rose, creating a reservoir eleven miles long and one mile wide at the widest point and consisting of 6,700 lake acres. The new reservoir impounded about thirty-five billion gallons of water at capacity.[49]

The regulating district declared the new dam an immediate success. They claimed to have finally ended destructive floods on the Beaver River and achieved a reasonable annual flow rate. Businesses on the Black River now had a steady supply of water and could run year-round where previously they had operated in only the spring and fall.

The 1924 Stillwater dam is still in service. Along with a number of newer downstream dams, it provides electricity and regulates the flow of the Beaver River. The dam was last renovated in 2001. In order to accomplish this work, the dam gates were completely opened and the entire reservoir drained for one summer season. The original course of the Beaver River reappeared. A century's worth of treasure and junk was exposed and rediscovered.

# 9

# Dr. Webb and His Railroad

Creation of the Stillwater Reservoir was not the only development that altered the Beaver River country forever. In late 1892, the Mohawk and Malone (M&M) Railroad opened for business, connecting the upper Beaver River with the outside world. The arduous trip to the sportsman's paradise that had formerly taken days suddenly could be comfortably made in hours. The story of the creation of the railroad and the resulting changes to the Beaver River country is central to understanding the future course of the region.

### The M&M Steams Through

William Seward Webb was born in New York City on January 31, 1851.[1] In 1861 his family moved to Rio de Janeiro when his father, James Watson Webb, was appointed US ambassador to Brazil.[2] In 1863 Seward, as his family called him, returned to the United States to attend boarding school at Colonel Churchill's Military Academy in Sing Sing (now Ossining), New York. He graduated after five years and entered the medical course at Columbia College, but he left Columbia in 1871 to study medicine in Paris and Vienna. After two years he returned to America, where he graduated from the Columbia University College for Physicians and Surgeons in 1875.

In 1881, Webb married Eliza "Lila" Osgood Vanderbilt, the youngest daughter of William H. Vanderbilt, president of the New York Central Railroad. At the behest of his wife's family, Dr. Webb closed his medical practice and became a partner in the Wall Street firm of Worden and Co.[3]

31. Portrait of Dr. William Seward Webb, uncredited photograph. Wallace, *Guide*, p. 422.

In 1883, Webster Wagner, the president of the Wagner Palace Car Company, was crushed to death between two of his own luxury railroad cars. William H. Vanderbilt owned a controlling interest in the company, and thanks to his father-in-law's influence, Seward Webb was selected the new president of the company in 1885. He remained in charge of that business until it was merged with the Pullman Company in 1899.

In 1890, William H. Vanderbilt announced plans to construct a New York Central rail line connecting to Canada. This must have puzzled competitors because the only available route had to cross the Adirondacks. The tremendous expense of building such a line appeared to make it untenable. The next year the New York Central purchased the Rome, Watertown & Ogdensburg Railroad (RW&O), which skirted the Adirondacks to the west, thereby saving itself the expense of building a new line, or so it seemed.

Dr. Webb was not involved with the management of the New York Central but was certainly aware of the importance of Canadian trade. Even though New York Central trains could now reach Canada by going around the Adirondacks on the RW&O line, Webb had a better idea. If a more direct line could be built across the west central Adirondacks, he reasoned that not only would the passenger business be quite profitable, but new freight opportunities would also open up.[4] Webb decided to personally finance and build just such a new line.[5]

Webb started to obtain the necessary right-of-way in early 1891. In the Beaver River country, he acquired 350,000 acres in a single purchase from the Adirondack Timber and Mineral Company. This purchase made Webb the owner of most of the land between the St. Lawrence County line and the Fulton Chain of Lakes, including most of the land surrounding the upper Beaver River.[6]

Webb actually began construction on separate portions of the projected railroad even before he had secured all the necessary right-of-way. He hired eight independent construction engineers to oversee work on each segment. Each of these engineers hired a number of construction companies to perform the actual work. Webb pushed the contractors hard. Working conditions were sometimes so bad that whole work gangs downed tools and walked off the job, only to be replaced by others. Some contractors hired experienced Mohawk railroad workers from the St. Regis Reservation near Massena. Other contractors favored Italian Americans. Some of the contractors brought in African American laborers from Tennessee. These southerners were experienced in railroad construction but ill-prepared to work outdoors in an Adirondack winter. The contractors apparently misrepresented both working conditions and wages to lure them north. The resulting labor troubles made headlines all across New York.[7]

The final spike was driven on October 12, 1892, at Twitchell Creek, not far from Stillwater. Scheduled passenger service began on October 24. In eighteen months, Webb's contractors had managed to lay 191 miles of track under extremely difficult conditions.

Webb named the completed line the Mohawk & Malone (M&M) Railway. Only a few months later, on April 20, 1893, he leased the M&M tracks to the New York Central. The southern terminal was shifted to Utica and the line renamed the Adirondack Division of the New York Central. This lease arrangement continued until January 1, 1905, when the New York Central purchased the M&M line outright, ending Dr. Webb's financial interest.[8]

As Webb predicted, the M&M attracted a substantial tourist trade. By 1910, ten passenger trains a day passed through Beaver River Station, although not all of them had scheduled stops. On Friday evenings in the summer months, the overnight sleeper to the Adirondacks would depart from New York City in five separate sections (five different trains). Each train had ten to fourteen cars with three hundred to four hundred passengers.[9]

## Nehasane, Dr. Webb's Private Preserve

Dr. Webb was already quite familiar with the charms of the Adirondack wilderness before he became involved in building his railroad line. In the early 1880s, Webb and his brother-in-law, Frederick W. Vanderbilt, along with a few friends, acquired a ten-thousand-acre plot a few miles outside of Tupper Lake, which they named the Kildare Club. Their preserve was reached on a sixteen-mile private dirt road through nearly virgin forest. Members originally slept in tents that were later replaced by fine buildings.[10] Webb went to the Kildare Club regularly for fishing and hunting throughout the 1880s.[11]

It is easy to imagine that Dr. Webb saw building a railroad through the west-central Adirondacks not only as a profit-making venture in itself but also as a way to acquire his own private wilderness retreat. After the railroad was complete, he still owned about 120,000 acres around the upper Beaver River from the St. Lawrence County line all the way to the Fulton Chain of Lakes. As explained earlier, Webb's plan for this property was to reserve forty thousand acres around Smith's Lake for his own exclusive use and to harvest timber from the rest. After the timber was cut down, Webb planned to divide the lakeside property along the Fulton Chain and at Big Moose Lake into cottage lots for sale to the public.[12]

He named his forty-thousand-acre private preserve Ne-Ha-Sa-Ne Park, after the original Mohawk name for the Beaver River.[13] At the center of his preserve lay Smith's Lake, the famous destination of the old-time sportsmen. As a tribute to his wife, Webb renamed it Lake Lila, and decided to build his Great Camp on the site of Lamont's hotel. He hired architect Robert Robinson to design a complex of buildings including a main lodge, two train stations, eleven sleeping cabins, and two boathouses, all in a sophisticated shingle style.[14] When these buildings were completed in 1893, Webb named the main building Forest Lodge. It had room for twenty-five guests, including

32. At Lake Lila, Hamilton County, showing Webb's Forest Lodge, photograph by J. M. Schuler. *Annual Report of the Forest Commission for the Year 1894*, facing p. 250.

space to accommodate eight to ten guides. There were separate quarters for the ten full-time staff. Webb's Great Camp eventually had eighty-six ancillary buildings.[15]

Webb was a dedicated sportsman. He especially loved hunting. Although whitetail deer were plentiful along the upper Beaver River, Webb wanted his guests to have a more varied hunting experience. Accordingly, he had his gamekeepers construct a ten-foot-high wire fence around ten thousand acres near Lake Lila to create a private game preserve. Over the next decade he variously stocked the preserve with moose, elk, caribou, English stags, black-tailed deer, wild boar, and other game animals. In 1903, the threat of forest fires caused Dr. Webb to dismantle the fence and set the remaining animals free.[16]

As explained fully in the previous chapter, Dr. Webb sold seventy-five thousand acres of forest to the state of New York in 1895 to settle the lawsuit he brought because the 1894 Stillwater dam blocked his use of the Beaver River for floating logs to market. While this sale prevented much of the area from being logged, there were still a large number of acres of timber he intended to harvest.

To his credit, Dr. Webb was one of the first large Adirondack landowners to argue that wilderness preservation and timber harvesting could successfully coexist. Webb was convinced that scientific lumbering practices would allow for natural reforestation and actually improve the health of the forest.[17] He hired one of the early proponents of selective cutting, Gifford Pinchot, to conduct a timber survey of his Beaver River lands.[18] Pinchot provided Webb with a scientific forest management plan.[19] Webb hired three different lumber contractors to harvest selected timber, mostly spruce, on widely separated parts of his property.[20]

One of those lumber contractors was Firman Ouderkirk, owner of successful lumber mills in southern Herkimer County. Ouderkirk agreed to build a sawmill near the new Beaver River Station to process logs cut from Webb lands. An important part of Ouderkirk's business was sawing spruce butts for pianos and violin sounding boards.[21] His mill started to operate in 1893.

## Six-Tenths of a Square Mile

Dr. Webb directed a train station for the Beaver River country be built where an old logging tote road crossed the tracks about two and a half miles west of Little Rapids.[22] At the time there were no dwellings or other buildings at the location. His construction crews cleared a few acres and built a station and some outbuildings.[23] By building a station several miles away from his Great Camp, he felt the public could be safely diverted away from Nehasane Park.[24]

To further assure that the common tourist would not be able to disembark at either of the two stations on his private preserve, Nehasane and Keepawa, Webb arranged that his invited guests would have to possess a signed "stop permit." These permits could be acquired only from Webb or his staff. As an example of his sense of humor, and as a none-too-subtitle hint to tourists, Webb made sure train conductors pronounced Keepawa station as "keep away."

Webb felt sure that someday there would be a need for private land in the vicinity of the new Beaver River station to build a

**STOP PERMIT**

NE-HA-SA-NE PARK

Upon presentation of this permit in connection with regular railroad fares or ticket conductors are authorized to let bearer off at Nehasane or Keepawa. This permit must be shown to station agent at starting point.

Issued to ...................................................

NEHASANE PARK ASS'N

Per .............................................

NOT GOOD AFTER ....................................

33. Stop permit for Nehasane Park's private train stations, one item in a collection of stationary and permits, Control #15199 Image file 042\15199.JPG. Courtesy of the Adirondack Experience.

settlement. Therefore, in 1893 Webb arranged for a survey of a square parcel of land exactly six-tenths of a mile on each side, more or less centered on the station. Webb's new Beaver River Block was comprised of Lot 51 of Township Forty-Two of the Totten and Crossfield Purchase and an adjoining strip of John Brown's Tract Township Number Five.

In 1896, Webb sold most of his land surrounding the upper Beaver River to New York State but reserved the Beaver River Block and forty thousand acres at his private Nehasane Park. From that time on Beaver River Station has been a 384-acre island of private property in a sea of state Forest Preserve. At the time of the sale, Webb arranged that two existing roads, the one to Grassy Point and the segment of the Carthage-to-Lake Champlain Road leading to Stillwater, would remain open to the public.[25] Another stipulation of the sale was that the three existing lumber contracts could continue until their expiration dates. When Ouderkirk's lumber contract expired in 1899, he purchased the entire Beaver River Block in order to protect his ongoing sawmill business.[26]

By the beginning of the twentieth century, most of the defining characteristics of today's Beaver River country were coming into focus. The state had already begun the process that would turn the great marsh of the Beaver River into the Stillwater Reservoir. The state had also acquired much of the forest around the upper Beaver River and added it to the Forest Preserve, thus protecting it from logging and further sale. Opening up this land to the public attracted a new cadre of tourists who could gain convenient access by railroad. Finally, a small area of private property was available for purchase at Beaver River Station.

# 10

# Beaver River Station

The six-tenths of a square mile where the settlement of Beaver River stands today was uninhabited before the railroad started to operate at the end of 1892. The old Carthage-to-Lake Champlain Road passed nearby but was not used by many travelers. Logging was going on at a few locations nearby. A rough logging tote road ran to the Beaver River from a lumber camp a short distance back in the forest. Otherwise, the wilderness was undisturbed.

In the days before the railroad, sporting tourists had no reason to stop there. Almost all of them were bound for Smith's Lake. If they stopped at all, it was to spend the night at Chauncey Smith's log cabin, located at what was called the Sand Spring near the confluence of the South Branch with the main Beaver River. After 1878 they could also stop at Muncy's Hotel at Little Rapids. When they arrived at Smith's Lake, they could camp at one of the established clearings or, after 1878, stay at the Smith's Lake Hotel (Lamont's).

All of this changed when Dr. Webb acquired the land surrounding the eastern end of the Beaver River in 1891. As noted, Webb had no intention of allowing unrestricted sporting tourism on his property, especially around Smith's and Albany lakes.[1] He immediately closed both Lamont's and Muncy's Hotels, posted no trespassing signs, and completely closed off public access to the upper end of the Beaver River. To further prevent trespassing, he hired fourteen to sixteen private game protectors.[2] Almost overnight the favored hunting and fishing grounds at the headwaters of the Beaver River became inaccessible to the sporting tourists who had camped there for decades.[3]

The very next year, in late 1892, a group of businessmen purchased and closed Dunbar's Hotel to create their private Beaver River Club (see chapter 11). They leased an additional six thousand acres in the Stillwater area and posted it against trespass.

Dr. Webb and the founders of the Beaver River Club were aware that by closing off their land they would encounter some resentment from nearby residents and a small band of sporting tourists. Both were careful to advertise that the public could have access to their private preserves on application.[4] In reality, most everyone knew that applying for permission to camp, fish, or hunt on either preserve was futile.

The local guides who previously worked out of Fenton's, Dunbar's, Muncy's, and Lamont's temporarily lost a source of income, but many were soon hired by Webb or the Beaver River Club. Even so, resentment over the posting of land previously open to everyone ran deep. no trespassing signs disappeared frequently and other minor acts of vandalism were common. Sometimes, angry locals took more extreme actions such as intentionally setting forest fires and in one case even the murder of a wealthy landowner.[5]

### Sportsmen's Paradise

In 1893 it may have seemed that the Beaver River country was destined to become a private park for the wealthy. Then came the 1894 dam, and by the end of 1895 the state had purchased seventy-five thousand acres formerly owned by Webb and reopened it to the public.

Almost immediately, sportsmen from all over New York State found themselves wanting to visit the new state land for fishing and hunting. It was a simple matter to purchase a train ticket to Beaver River Station. As the tide of sporting tourists started to rise, local guides and entrepreneurs developed accommodations for them. As a result, between 1895 and 1925 the Beaver River country became a sportsmen's paradise.

Beaver River Station was quite an interesting place in those days. At the railroad station it was possible to encounter people from at least four different social classes. There was the occasional person of great

wealth from one of the East Coast cities traveling to or from Dr. Webb's
Great Camp Nehasane. More frequently there would be a well-to-do
upstate family traveling to or from the Beaver River Club. The most
frequent visitors were upstate professional men of moderate means who
stayed at a hotel in or near Beaver River Station or at a camp on the Red
Horse Chain. The fourth group was made up of the guides, hotel workers, and laborers, along with a few sawmill workers and lumberjacks.

The sporting tourists who stayed in or around Beaver River Station
were small business owners, successful tradesmen, doctors, lawyers, and
other professionals. Like the sporting tourists who came before them,
they were attracted by the outdoor life centered on fishing and hunting. At first the men came by themselves just for fishing and hunting,
but as facilities developed, their wives and families came, too. As their
numbers increased, so did the number of facilities that catered to them.

### Elliott Camp: ~1893–1912

The first accommodation for sportsmen built in the vicinity of the new
Beaver River Station was the Elliott Camp. Located directly on the
Beaver River not far from its junction with the South Branch, Elliott's
was a typical two-story sportsmen's hotel with cedar shake siding.

Chester J. "Chet" Elliott was born in 1853. His wife, Addie Odett,
was born in 1856. They married in 1879. They had three children:
William, Joseph, and Jessie. Every spring and fall throughout the
1880s, Chet Elliott and his brother William worked for their uncle
Joe Dunbar at the Dunbar Hotel at Stillwater. After Dunbar sold the
hotel, he helped his nephews build the Elliott Camp, probably during 1893. Chet and his brother William initially operated the Elliott
Camp together with Chet's wife, Addie, doing the cooking. William
soon found a job at a hotel in Lowville and moved to town.[6]

Chet Elliott became quite the wilderness entrepreneur. He met
every train driving his wagon and team. If visitors were bound for the
Beaver River Club, he would drive them about a mile to Grassy Point,
where he kept a small homemade side-wheel steamboat docked on the
river. The little boat ferried visitors in relative comfort to the club at

34. Elliott's Camp, Beaver River, New York, undated photo postcard by Henry M. Beach. Courtesy of Frank Carey.

Stillwater. He named his steamboat *Wild Jess* after his adventurous daughter.[7]

All three of the Elliott children grew up experienced in the ways of the wilderness. As early as 1898 the two Elliott boys, especially Will, were praised for their skill as guides.[8] Eighteen-year-old Jessie was featured in a lengthy article that recounts a weeklong stay at Elliott's Camp in 1903. "Miss Jessie" was described as an attractive young woman who "will serve you at meal time with flap-jacks, venison and coffee, take your photograph, beat you shooting, run a foot race, paddle a canoe, spring tricks on you at camp-fire, or teach a Sunday school class."[9]

For a few years the Elliott Camp was the only place a visitor could stay in the vicinity of the Beaver River train station. The camp prospered. Chet improved the main building and added a dozen cabins along the riverbank. Newspapers from all over upstate New York carried favorable articles about successful fishing and hunting expeditions based at Elliott's.[10]

In the spring of 1912, after twenty successful years, Chet Elliott sold the camp to W. H. and C. B. Johnson.[11] The Elliott family moved to Carter Station, a small railroad community closer to Old Forge, and took over management of the Clearwater House.[12]

*Camps along the Red Horse Trail: 1896–1916*

Shortly after 1896, when the state acquired the Webb lands around the Beaver River, a number of local outdoors guides erected sportsmen's camps on the north side of the river along the Red Horse Trail. They did not bother to seek permission from the state because for decades squatting had been a common practice by guides. Even though the Forest Commission identified squatting as one of its most pressing concerns as early as 1891, eviction proved to be difficult. For decades the Forest Commission adopted a policy of benign neglect.[13] After 1901 they regularly sent squatters eviction notices, but no serious legal action was taken against squatters in the Beaver River country until 1915.

Some of the Red Horse Trail camps consisted of nothing more than a simple open camp or lean-to. Others were log cabins or small frame

35. Charlie Smith's camp at Salmon Lake, uncredited photo postcard. Courtesy of Timothy Mayers.

hotels. Perhaps the most well known of these Red Horse camps was Elmer Wilder's Camp Happy on Salmon Lake.[14] Other early camps on Salmon Lake included the Lansing Hotaling Camp, the Cobb Camp, the Townsend Camp, and the Charlie Smith Camp. Dave Conkey's, Chris Wagner's, and the Greely camps were all located on Big Burnt Lake.[15] The Stanton camps were on the north side of the Beaver River about three miles west of the Big Burnt outlet.[16]

### The Original Norridgewock Hotel: 1899–1914

Firman Ouderkirk, the lumberman, built the original Norridgewock Hotel in 1899.[17] The original Norridgewock sat on the west side of the railroad tracks. A paved sidewalk led straight from the station to the hotel. It was a grand Victorian edifice with room for up to one hundred guests.[18] Ouderkirk hired Berdett "Bert" B. Bullock, son of Monroe "Pop" Bullock, as his hotel manager.

There is no record of why Ouderkirk chose to name his hotel the Norridgewock. Norridgewock is the anglicized version of the Abenaki

36. The original Norridgewock Hotel, undated photo postcard by Henry M. Beach. Courtesy of Frank Carey.

Indian word *Nanrantswak*. It was originally the name of a band of
Abenaki Indians that inhabited the Kennebec River Valley in Maine.
The literal translation of the name is "people of the still water between
rapids."[19] As it happened, the two most famous nineteenth-century
guides in the central Adirondacks, Mitchel Sabattis and Lewis Elijah
Benedict, were both Norridgewock Indians.[20] It seems plausible that
Ouderkirk decided to use an authentic Abenaki name for his hotel as
his way of paying tribute to these two famous guides.

The hotel did very well thanks to the ever-increasing number of
sporting tourists arriving on the train. In 1902, with his lumber business winding down, Ouderkirk sold the entire Beaver River block,
including the Norridgewock, to the hotel manager Bert Bullock. The
hotel continued to flourish. By 1907 Bullock had hired Louis Beach,
a skilled Lowville carpenter and all-round handyman.[21] By 1909 the
hotel was doing well enough that Bullock was able to build a large
concrete block stable across the Grassy Point Road from the hotel.
He also added piped-in water and hired a small orchestra to entertain
guests. Bert himself played cornet.[22] As proof of his pride in owner-
ship, Bullock commissioned a fancy nickel-plated cash register embla-
zoned with his name.[23]

Louis Beach bought a lot and built his own camp near the hotel.
He eventually came to share hotel management duties with Bert Bullock. Business continued to be strong. Then on May 8, 1914, a fierce
fire burned the original Norridgewock Hotel to the ground. Bert
Bullock and his family had apparently had enough of backwoods living and decided not to rebuild. The family moved to Thendara, where
Bert opened a garage and taxi service.

*The Grassy Point Inn: 1901–24*

Bert Bullock's father, Monroe "Pop" Bullock, had worked as the manager of the Beaver River Club since 1893. His wife, Sarah Bullock,
died in 1901. Pop Bullock was apparently not able to manage the Beaver River Club without her help, so he resigned. With the assistance of
Bert, he built a small hotel at Grassy Point along the bank of the Beaver

37. Grassy Point Inn on Beaver River, uncredited photo postcard. Courtesy of Frank Carey.

River. He recruited a young woman from his hometown of Worth, New York, named Delia Weaver, to serve as cook and housekeeper.[24]

The Grassy Point Inn became an important waystation for many visitors. Anyone bound for the camps along the Red Horse Trail would have to take a boat across the river from Grassy Point. Members and guests of the Beaver River Club at Stillwater caught the club steamer at Grassy Point. Outdoors guides stored their boats and gear at Bullock's Inn. Pop Bullock may have made as much money transporting visitors and luggage back and forth from the train station in his buckboard as he made from renting rooms.

By the time the original Norridgewock burned in 1914, Pop Bullock was such a confirmed woodsman that he decided to stay in Beaver River when his son's family moved to town. Even when the state evicted him from Grassy Point in 1916, he dismantled his hotel, hauled it to a lot he owned near the railroad station, and resumed business. Pop and Delia continued to run the hotel, complete with store and post office, until 1923. At seventy-seven years of age, Pop sold the hotel to George Vincent. He and Delia moved in with Bert's family in Thendara.

Vincent's Hotel specifically catered to loggers. Vincent himself also worked a logging contract for pulpwood near Woods Lake.[25] Unfortunately, in May 1924 Vincent's newly acquired hotel burned to the ground. George Vincent and a guest, Mrs. Amos de Chambeau, perished in the fire.[26]

*Darrow's Sportsman's Lodge: 1909–45*

The Beaver River sportsmen's hotels built prior to 1916 were constructed on state land a fair distance from the station. Darrow's Sportsman's Lodge was the sole exception to this rule. In 1909, Albert "Burt" Darrow and his wife Ella built a modest boardinghouse on private land just east of the station.[27] Burt Darrow worked in the woods; Ella Darrow, called Aunt Ella by her guests, ran the hotel. In 1912 Burt even served for a year as Beaver River's first Forest Ranger.[28] It was Ella's usual practice to close her boardinghouse in the winter and move to Brandreth to work as a cook in the lumber camps.[29]

38. Darrow's Cottages, Beaver River, New York, uncredited photo postcard. Courtesy of Frank Carey and the Norridgewock Lodge.

During the early 1920s, accommodations in Beaver River Station were in high demand by those working on the reservoir project. During this time Darrow's expanded and additional buildings were constructed. Ella Darrow was busy enough that she needed to hire help. A fellow from Canada, Edwin Butcher, became her right-hand man. Butcher built his camp on a lot next to Darrow's.[30]

Burt Darrow died in 1924. After the reservoir was completed in 1925, Darrow's became an island reached on a floating bridge. Ella Darrow continued to operate the hotel until it burned down in 1945.[31]

### Loon Lake Lodge / The Evergreen: 1911–20

In 1911, Bill and Hattie Thompson and their two sons moved to a camp on state land at Loon Lake, a pretty body of water on the south side of the Beaver River about halfway to Stillwater along the Carthage-to-Lake Champlain Road.[32] They came from Sperryville, a small settlement near Chase Lake in the Town of Watson where Hattie was a schoolteacher. The Loon Lake Lodge was the Thompsons' entry into

39. Loon Lake Camp near Beaver River, New York, uncredited photo postcard. Courtesy of Timothy Mayers.

the tourist trade, beginning the family's more than one-hundred-year tenure as Beaver River hotel keepers.[33] Bill Thompson died not long after moving to the Beaver River country but Hattie, with the help of her sons, Clint and Walter, continued to operate the lodge. In 1916 they dismantled the lodge, reconstructed it on a lot in Beaver River Station, and renamed it The Evergreen. They continued to serve visitors until 1920 when Clint and Walter purchased the Norridgewock II.

### Oasis in the Wilderness[34]

During the first decade of the twentieth century there was little interest in building adjacent to the Beaver River station. The original Norridgewock Hotel provided everything needed for visitors who wanted a taste of the wilderness with all the amenities. Those seriously interested in fishing and hunting were accommodated in the outlying guides' camps. Those camps, with the single exception of Darrow's, were all illegally located on state Forest Preserve land.

No effective action was taken to remove these trespassers until the fall of 1915. After years of benign neglect, the Conservation Commission finally decided to crack down on illegal occupation of state land throughout the Adirondacks. All squatters were served with formal eviction notices that they must immediately remove their possessions or have them destroyed.[35] By the fall of 1917, all the sportsmen's camps on state land around the Beaver River were gone. Only two hotels, Thompson's and Bullock's, relocated into Beaver River Station. Beaver River Camps (the former Elliott's), Wilder's Camp Happy, and all the other outlying camps were demolished.[36] As a result, by the end of 1917 the little settlement of Beaver River Station had four hotels: Darrow's, Bullock's, The Evergreen, and the Norridgewock II.

### *The Norridgewock II and III*

After the original Norridgewock was destroyed by fire, Bert Bullock sold the section of the Beaver River Block on the west side of the railroad tracks where the hotel had been to Albert S. Hosley of Tupper

Lake. He sold the property on the east side of the tracks to the Beaver River Camp Site Co. Both new owners filed subdivision maps with hopes of selling lots for camps and cottages.[37]

With the original Norridgewock gone, there was a strong demand for more lodging. In 1917, Peter Propp bought the parcel on the west side of the tracks from Hosley. Instead of building a completely new hotel, Propp converted the existing large stable into a hotel by adding a second story with six bedrooms. A two-story addition was attached to the rear, with a dining room and parlor on the first floor and five bedrooms on the second. Louis Beach was involved in the construction and leased the hotel from Propp as soon as it was complete.[38] Lou Beach called the new hotel the Norridgewock, continuing the well-known name. In time it became known as the Norridgewock II.

40. Norridgewock II in 1917. Group of hunters with Henry M. Beach first from left; son Harry Beach at far right. Gelatin silver print, photographer unknown. Printed verso in pen and ink: "1917." ADKX #PO42330, Catalog #1978.053.0117. Courtesy of the Adirondack Experience.

In 1920, Clinton and Walter Thompson, the grown sons of Bill and Hattie Thompson, purchased the Norridgewock II. Lou Beach sold his camp and moved to Old Forge, where he found work as a carpenter. Over the next number of years, the Thompson brothers purchased much of the property of original Beaver River Block.[39] About 1924 the Thompson brothers built a general store, called the Annex, on the site of the original Norridgewock[40] because that spring Vincent's Hotel, which contained the settlement's general store and post office, burned to the ground.

Clint Thompson married Jennie Shaw from Lowville, and in time they had three children: Stanley, Lucille, and Marion. Walter Thompson married Gladys Kempton. Walter and Gladys ran the general store and post office[41] in the Annex. They lived upstairs from the store with their six children.[42]

The Thompson brothers' partnership dissolved in 1939 when Walter and Gladys moved to Fort Edward, New York, near the Vermont border.[43] Clint purchased his brother's share of the business and converted the upstairs of the Annex into extra hotel rooms for the Norridgewock II.[44] Clint and Jennie continued to successfully operate the Norridgewock II with the help of their children until Clint died in 1964.

Clint Thompson died without a will. Stanley Thompson, Clint and Jennie's son, had for some years been deeply involved running the Norridgewock II with his wife, Pat Morran. They wanted to continue, but his mother and sisters wanted to move elsewhere. As a result, the Norridgewock II closed.[45] The Thompson property was divided, with Stanley getting the land on the east side of the tracks and his mother and two sisters getting the land on the west side, including the Norridgewock II.[46]

Stanley and Pat were determined to continue to operate a hotel in Beaver River Station. Even though the railroad had stopped carrying passengers in 1964, the community now had a considerable number of

41. The Norridgewock Lodge as it appeared in 2021. Courtesy of the Norridgewock Lodge.

seasonal residents who arrived by boat, plus a steady winter clientele of snowmobilers.[47] Accordingly, the Thompsons built a new hotel on the property east of the railroad tracks. The Norridgewock III opened for business at its current location in the spring of 1965.[48] The Thompsons later bought the adjacent Terry cabin and added a six-room motel unit to provide more lodging.[49]

On March 1, 1974, the Norridgewock III burned to the ground, but was quickly rebuilt as it exists today with the help of many volunteers.[50] It reopened in July 1974. It has been open ever since. The children of Stanley and Pat Thompson later inherited the property. In 2017 the Thompson family was able to purchase and renovate the Norridgewock II to use for group functions.

## *The Roaring Twenties*

Beaver River Station had thirty residents in 1920, according to the US Census. Fourteen more lived at the nearby Stillwater Lumber Camp. These loggers were the vanguard of a new temporary logging boom. Between 1920 and 1924, New York State hired a number of logging contractors to completely clear more than four thousand acres of land that would soon be flooded by the new reservoir. Local men from all over the Adirondacks headed for Beaver River to work alongside large groups of French-Canadian lumberjacks.

The loggers took up residence not only in logging camps but also at the Norridgewock II, Darrow's, and Bullock's. Some slept in open shanties or in tents. The *Utica Observer Dispatch* described the scene as more like the Wild West than New York State "with its rough, crude surroundings and several hundred French Canadian huskies living in tumble down shacks—or some of them with bare ground for a bed and the sky for a roof."[51]

Although Prohibition became the law of the land in 1920, it took quite a while for this news to reach the Beaver River country. Several small lunchrooms or cafes serving illegal booze sprang up in Beaver River to cater to the thirsty loggers. Things got so rough and rowdy that the New York State police stationed three troopers there to keep law and order.[52]

Jessie Elliott, who grew up at Elliott's Camp, returned to Beaver River Station in 1921 with her husband, Harry Smith. Jessie met Harry when they worked together as cooks at George Bushey's lumber camp at nearby Woods Lake. Harry Smith operated one of the infamous Beaver River lunchrooms. In late October 1923, federal agents staged a raid and arrested Harry after he was observed selling illegal whiskey. Harry pled not guilty. He must have been let off with just a fine because in 1924 he was arrested again for the same offense.[53] His second offense probably drew a stiffer penalty because there is no record of Harry ever appearing in Beaver River or Jessie's life again.[54]

When the dam that created the current Stillwater Reservoir was put into service in 1925, a significant portion of the east end of the Beaver River Block surrounding the South Branch disappeared under water. Seven Beaver River camps were relocated to higher ground.[55] The New York State Census for 1925 shows ninety people residing in Beaver River Station, but fifty of them were railroad workers rebuilding a section of collapsed track. By 1930, the US Census found the population had shrunk to thirty-nine. The stationmaster, Bill Partridge, had seven children, so this one family constituted a quarter of the population. By 2019, the settlement had grown to include about one hundred seasonal camps but had a year-round population of only four, all members of the Thompson family.

# Part Four

# Private Clubs

42. Summer party at the Beaver River Clubhouse about 1910, undated photo postcard attributed to Henry M. Beach, Rap-Shaw Photo Album image 1-23. Courtesy of the Rap-Shaw Club, Inc.

43. Rap-Shaw Club Witchhopple Lake Camp, large family gathering, about 1910, uncredited photograph, Rap-Shaw Photo Album image MW-04. Courtesy of the Rap-Shaw Club, Inc.

# 11

# The Beaver River Club

## The Rise of Private Sportsmen's Clubs

Historians have paid a good deal of attention to the acquisition of large tracts of land and the building of grand rustic family compounds by the super-wealthy of the time.[1] William Seward Webb's Nehasane Park is a good example of the sort of Adirondack wilderness retreat coveted by a number of leading financiers and industrialists from East Coast cities. By the end of the nineteenth century, some of the most picturesque locations could boast one of these enclaves.

While the so-called Great Camps are certainly one of the distinctive features of late nineteenth-century Adirondack history, they involved only a small number of visitors. A far more important development and one with more long-lasting impact on the course of Adirondack history was the rise of private sportsmen's clubs.[2]

The tourists who frequented the new hotels along the edges of the Adirondacks after 1870 were financially well-off. They were wealthy enough to afford to take several weeks or a month off work. They could afford the cost of travel, lodging, and hiring a guide. Such costs were beyond the means of most working men and women, but not beyond the means of doctors, lawyers, ministers, store owners, professional tradesmen, and similar community leaders.

Some of these tourists were so enchanted by the Adirondack wilderness that they wanted to build their own vacation retreat in the woods. Because they were not incredibly wealthy, the only way they could amass sufficient resources to realize their dream was to band together to form a club.[3]

The aim of all these clubs was similar. They would cooperatively purchase or lease a large parcel of Adirondack wilderness where only club members could hunt and fish. On part of this land, they typically built a substantial main lodge where club members could sleep and take their meals. The adjoining land was sold or leased to members who wished to build their own private cottages. By providing meals for members, the clubs solved the significant problem of individuals transporting heavy kitchen gear and food into the woods. Sportsmen's clubs usually were able to hire guides who knew the area well, thus avoiding the perceived incompetence of the "hotel" guides generally available to tourists.[4]

The New York state legislature saw the benefit of encouraging the development of sportsmen's clubs. "An Act for Private Parks and Game Preserves" of 1871 allowed the posting of private lands as game preserves and lease of land to private clubs. Because the clubs usually hired local guides to patrol their land to keep out trespassers, in 1892 the state amended the law to explicitly allow employees of sportsmen's clubs to arrest trespassers.

Sportsmen's clubs proliferated throughout the Adirondacks in the years between 1870 and 1900. The *Report of the Forest Commission for 1893* contained a list of all known private clubs.[5] By that year fifty private clubs owned outright or leased an aggregate total of 940,000 acres, nearly one quarter of the entire Adirondack Park. The report praised the clubs because the Forest Commission believed they were good stewards of the land, with the added benefit of posing no cost to the state.

The first sportsmen's club established in the Beaver River country was called the Smith's Lake Park Association. William Morrison, a businessman from Lowville, founded this club in January 1891.[6] Morrison purchased most of the land surrounding Smith's Lake and part of Albany Lake on behalf of his friends who had been visiting the area for many years on hunting and fishing trips. Morrison had plans to enlarge Lamont's Hotel, recruit new members, and possibly establish a fish hatchery. He even went to the considerable expense of installing a telephone line linking Smith's Lake with Lowville.

The Smith's Lake Park Association only survived for five months. In June 1891, Dr. Webb purchased Morrison's property as a part of his plan to establish his Great Camp, Nehasane.[7]

## Heyday of the Beaver River Club

The members of the short-lived Smith's Lake Park Association had no intention of abandoning their favorite vacationland. They all were familiar with the advantages of the Dunbar Hotel at Stillwater. As it happened, Joe Dunbar was ready to retire. In December 1892, thirty-two well-to-do businessmen primarily from Syracuse, Utica, and Lowville, led by William Morrison and William Moshier, purchased the Dunbar Hotel.[8] They also purchased all of Dunbar's property, plus an additional fifty acres to increase their holdings to two hundred acres. They also signed a multiyear lease for six thousand additional acres of forest and lakes in the immediate vicinity.[9]

On February 10, 1893, they formally founded the Beaver River Club. They renamed Dunbar's Hotel the Beaver River Clubhouse and hired Monroe "Pop" Bullock, a well-regarded local guide who we met in an earlier chapter, to manage it. The new club property contained three hills connected by the old Carthage-to-Lake Champlain Road. Most of the property was a low-lying meadow. The Dunbar Hotel sat on top of the easternmost hill, surrounded by a number of cabins and two boathouses.

When the 1894 dam was completed, the entire property became a beautiful two-hundred-acre island. The new club had their island surveyed and divided into cottage lots for sale to prospective members. The original map drawn by S. S. Snell shows fifty-two cottage lots as well as building lots on four nearby islands.[10] The Snell map shows the location of the clubhouse on the right side of the road, along with a laundry, icehouse, and barn.

The new Beaver River Club appears on the list of sportsmen's clubs found in the *Report of the Forest Commission for 1893*. The report describes how members of the Beaver River Club and guests could reach the remote club by wagon, traveling the last twelve miles "through

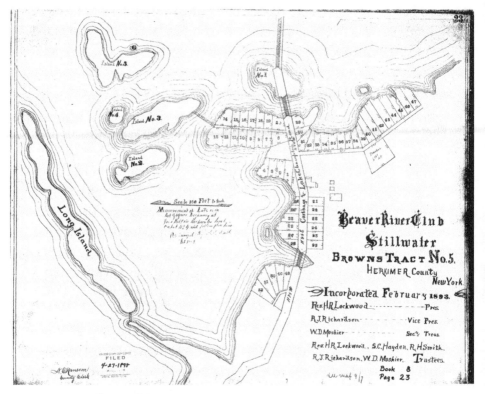

44. 1893 Snell map of the Beaver River Club, Herkimer Co. Clerk's Office, Book 8 of maps, p. 23, filed Apr. 27, 1898.

unbroken wilderness" along the Carthage-to-Lake Champlain Road from Number Four, or by rail to Beaver River Station and then by boat to Stillwater. The report also claims that the original membership of thirty-five had already grown to fifty families who stayed in cottages on waterfront lots. These numbers were aspirational. Review of maps, land records, and tax records does not support that membership ever exceeded forty-two families. Only twenty-six lots were ever sold, and based on later maps it appears only fifteen cottages were actually built. Because the *Report of the Forest Commission for 1893* was the only published account of the Beaver River Club from those early days, it has been quoted as gospel over the years.[11]

45. 1902 Beaver River Club Clubhouse, uncredited photo postcard. Collection of the author.

The leaders of the Beaver River Club had grand plans. Beginning in 1900, they started to raise funds to enlarge or replace Dunbar's Hotel with a new structure that could seat eighty in the dining room.[12] The new clubhouse was completed by 1902 at a total cost of ten thousand dollars.[13] It is unclear from surviving photographs whether the original Dunbar's Hotel was demolished or just overshadowed by the larger new structure. To defray the cost of their new clubhouse, members were assessed annual dues for the first time.

At the same time, they commissioned a supplemental survey map of their property that increased the number of lots for sale from fifty-two to seventy-two.[14] These small lots of about one-quarter acre were being offered at $500–$600. When accounting for inflation, this means a lot cost about $12,000 in today's dollars.

The Beaver River Club soon became the favored wilderness retreat of many influential families. Although hunting and fishing were still part of the attraction, families also spent time boating, swimming, and socializing. Members brought servants and nannies to look after the children. In the evening, everyone dressed for dinner in only slightly less formal attire than they were accustomed to wear in the cities. And there were grand parties and picnics to which club members invited their city friends. One particularly remarkable party held at the club by Mr. and Mrs. Robert Dey in 1895 included fifty guests and featured the "novel amusement" of blowing soap bubbles.[15]

During its heyday, the membership rolls of the Beaver River Club read like the upstate social register. Successful manufacturers were well represented by men like William S. Foster of Utica, president of Foster Brothers Manufacturing, makers of iron beds and springs. From Syracuse there was Carlton A. Chase, president of Syracuse Chilled Plow and later president of the First Trust & Deposit Bank. Another prominent Syracuse civic leader was William K. Pierce, president of Pierce, Butler & Pierce, manufacturers of heating and plumbing fixtures. Pierce also founded the company that installed the first streetlights in Syracuse.

Large retailers and wholesalers were also well represented. Foremost among these was Robert Dey, founder and president of Dey Brothers department store, who is credited with inspiring the current Syracuse downtown shopping district. From Utica there was William D. Moshier, wholesaler of spices, extracts, and coffee.[16] A Lowville native, he joined the Beaver River Club with his brother and business partner Charles Moshier, his father John J. Moshier, and his brother-in-law A. C. Boshart. Also from Lowville were the Richardson brothers, who operated a grocery and drugstore and later developed a major wholesale trade in cheese and maple sugar.[17]

Professional men also made up a significant part of the membership. Chief among them was Syracuse attorney William P. Goodelle, known statewide for his legal work on behalf of the New York Central Railroad.[18] Goodelle served as club president from 1895 until at least 1910. The rector of St. Paul's Episcopal Church in Syracuse, Rev. Dr. Henry Lockwood, was a founding member. Leading physicians such as Dr. J. Willis Candee of Syracuse and Dr. Martin Besmer of Ithaca represented the medical profession.

To operate this elaborate club, the manager had to hire cooks, waitstaff, housemaids, fishing and hunting guides, and probably a few maintenance staff. Because there was no reasonably nearby town, hiring staff was a challenge. It appears the club hired seasonal employees

47. Portrait of William P. Goodelle from Stoddard, *Notable Men*, 29.

46. Portrait of William K. Pierce from Stoddard, *Notable Men*, 99.

48. Portrait of Rev. Henry R. Lockwood from Stoddard, *Notable Men*, 12.

from all around upstate and housed them on site. A newspaper article from July 1904 that reported the death of one Thomas Shaughnessy of Schenectady, age twenty-five, supports this surmise. Shaughnessy had been hired by the Beaver River Club but did not have the money for train fare. He was killed when he struck his head on a bridge while riding to Beaver River on top of a baggage car.[19]

The Beaver River Club truly flourished during the fifteen years from 1893 until 1908. In June 1902, H. C. (Henry Charles) Churchill replaced Pop Bullock as manager of the club. Churchill purchased a twenty-five-foot-long steamboat from D. H. Tuttle of Canastota, New York. He used this boat to transport Beaver River Club members in style from Grassy Point near Beaver River Station to the club dock on Twitchell Creek. Churchill named the steamer *Alice* in honor of his eldest daughter.

49. Boats at Grassy Point showing the steamer *Alice* and guideboats at low water, uncredited photograph from the Churchill-Shaver Album. Courtesy of Jim and Carol Fox.

Churchill decided to capitalize on the still-increasing flow of tourists to Stillwater. He could see there was a need for more accommodations, especially for tourists who did not wish to build their own camp. So, at the end of the season in 1905, he resigned as manager of the Beaver River Club in order to build his own hotel. That hotel, named the Old Homestead, opened the next spring near the west end of the first bridge to Dunbar Island[20] (see chapter 13). Local guide Harlow Young replaced Churchill as manager at the Beaver River Club.

Disaster struck the Beaver River Club on April 22, 1908, when the clubhouse burned to the ground in a fire that started in the kitchen. This was a devastating loss since all club members took their meals in the clubhouse and the summer season was about to begin. They all knew that the clubhouse needed to be rebuilt immediately if the Beaver River Club were to survive. Although he was the manager at the time, Harlow Young was not faulted. In fact, the club needed an experienced manager to direct the rebuilding.

The club was still doing quite well financially, so the board of directors decided to build a larger and more ornate replacement clubhouse.[21] The first floor would have a living room measuring thirty by forty feet, a spacious dining room, the kitchen, and a pantry. There would be eighteen bedrooms on the second floor and two indoor bathrooms. Wide porches would ring the north and east sides looking out on the mountains.

Unfortunately, the insurance proceeds from the loss of the first clubhouse were inadequate to completely finance this fine new hotel that would end up costing $20,000, or about $350,000 in today's dollars. To raise the necessary capital to rebuild, the Beaver River Club mortgaged the new clubhouse and all its remaining unsold real estate to Frederick William Barker Sr. of Syracuse for $12,000.[22] They reasoned that they could easily meet the mortgage payments out of room rentals and by selling more cottage lots.

The impressive new clubhouse was built in a rustic Queen Anne style during the next year and, at least for a while, all seemed well. Unfortunately, the club's finances began to fail. As early as 1910, the

50. The 1910 Beaver River Clubhouse, uncredited photograph from the Churchill-Shaver Album. Courtesy of Jim and Carol Fox.

club was behind on their mortgage payments. In an effort to raise cash they had Harlow Young distribute an advertising brochure to try to attract paying guests from the general public. They also hired another Beaver River guide, Carl McCormick, to aid in the effort.[23] In October 1910, club manager Harlow Young bought the Old Homestead Hotel (see chapter 13). He resigned as club manager and was replaced by Frank N. Williams of Watertown.[24]

The next summer, on June 11, 1911, as club members watched from the porch of a neighboring camp, lightning struck and destroyed the cottages of two leading Syracuse club members, James Belden and William Goodelle. Those two camps burned to the ground and were never rebuilt.[25]

This event seems to mark a further decline in the fortunes of the Beaver River Club. Perhaps it was the economy. Perhaps the club had counted on selling more lots but buyers never materialized. Perhaps the interests of the original members had shifted. Perhaps it was no longer as fashionable to take extended vacations in the Adirondacks.

Perhaps, perhaps, perhaps. Regardless of the cause, the club found it was unable to meet the costs of operating the clubhouse and paying the mortgage. After waiting a number of years for payment, Frederick Barker foreclosed.[26] The clubhouse and real estate of the Beaver River Club were sold at a referee's auction on December 18, 1914, to William S. Foster, Carlton A. Chase, and Charles S. Terry for $10,916.13, the amount still due on the mortgage.

This was not, however, the end of the Beaver River Club. The three men who purchased the property were all current members who owned cottages at the club. On December 28, 1914, these three and nine other members filed incorporation papers for a new sportsmen's club to be called the Stillwater Mountain Club. Although the Beaver River Club was not explicitly mentioned, the stated purpose of the new club was to "maintain a clubhouse in the Adirondacks."[27]

And so, the Beaver River Club continued to operate under a new organization. It does not appear that the name Stillwater Mountain Club was ever widely adopted. Maps drawn as late as 1924 continued to refer to the property as the Beaver River Club. There is no record that Foster, Chase, and Terry ever conveyed title to the land they purchased at the mortgage foreclosure to the Stillwater Mountain Club. These three continued to hold title jointly in their own names in hope that they could recoup their considerable investment through sale of more cottage lots.

### Flooding of the Club

Unfortunately, the new grand clubhouse did not bring about the expected increase in club membership. As early as the summer of 1911, usage of the Beaver River Club had begun to decline. After the mortgage foreclosure in 1914, few new cottage lots were sold and no new cottages built. By 1916 the club was renting the clubhouse to a guide named Bert A. Dobson. He circulated an advertising booklet for "Dobson's Beaver Island Camps" that rented rooms in the clubhouse to the public for twenty dollars per week including meals.[28] Dobson apparently rented the property for a few seasons, then left to operate his former camp near Wanakena.

Given all the public attention to dam-building in the Adirondacks, it seems fair to assume that during the later 1910s the possibility of a significant enlargement of the Stillwater dam became public knowledge. This would, of course, have alarmed the members of the Beaver River Club as almost all their property lay only a few feet above the existing water level. Some members, like investment banker Roger B. Williams Jr., appeared to believe that the higher dam would not be built and Beaver River Club would survive, but most of the club members held the view that a larger dam was inevitable. (See discussion in chapter 8.)

On November 29, 1919, as plans for the larger dam moved forward, the three co-owners of the clubhouse and the undeveloped land, Foster, Chase, and Terry, sold the property they had obtained at foreclosure in 1914 to Henry Wetmore. Wetmore operated the clubhouse on some basis for the next two years for those club members who continued to use their camps. Then, in April 1921 Wetmore sold the clubhouse and club lands to Henry J. McCormick. It is especially interesting that this sale also included all the boats, furnishings, and other personal property of the "former" Beaver River Club.[29] This suggests that by 1921 the Beaver River Clubhouse had been essentially abandoned.

The Black River Regulating District drew detailed maps of the area to be flooded by the larger reservoir.[30] These maps confirmed that almost all of the two hundred acres of the Beaver River Club, including the grand clubhouse and all but one of the member cottages, were in the area to be flooded.[31] The flooding would create two small islands suitable for habitation with a total of about five acres.

Two club members soon purchased these future islands. Arthur Virkler purchased about three quarters of an acre on the larger island and relocated his camp there. Roger Butler Williams Jr. purchased the remainder of that island as well as the smaller island just to its west. He built a family camp on the larger island by relocating some Beaver River Club buildings and salvaging others.[32]

On February 11, 1925, the gates closed at the new Stillwater dam and the water rose. Prior to the flooding, all club buildings were relocated or demolished to salvage any valuable materials. All that remained were the foundations.[33] In time, the once famous Beaver River Club faded into obscurity.

# 12

# The Rap-Shaw Club

### Founding the Rap-Shaw Club

In its early days, the Rap-Shaw Club was typical of many Adirondack sportsmen's clubs. Its members were middle-class business owners who banded together to share the costs and camaraderie of annual hunting and fishing trips. They established a fixed campsite and hired the same guides every season. Unlike most of the other late nineteenth-century sporting clubs, though, the Rap-Shaw Club still exists. This chapter tells the story of how the Rap-Shaw Club successfully made the transition from a male-only hunting and fishing club to the family outdoors club of today.[1]

According to the written reminiscence of John P. Rapalje, a founder and first president of the Rap-Shaw Club, it was the state's purchase of seventy-five thousand acres of wilderness land from Dr. Webb in January 1896 that first drew him to the Beaver River country.[2] Local, regional, and statewide sportsmen's organizations, newspapers, and sporting magazines regularly discussed fishing and hunting conditions in the Adirondacks. Sporting tourists all across the state were well aware that large tracts of the north woods were in private hands and closed off to the public. Accordingly, it was big news for sportsmen that a large tract of Adirondack wilderness was newly available for exploration.

Sportsmen like Rapalje were also attracted to the Beaver River because it had largely escaped the depletion of fish and game that was affecting the more accessible areas of the Adirondacks.[3] By the time the Rap-Shaw Club was founded, a combination of habitat destruction, market hunting, and unregulated sport hunting had profoundly reduced Adirondack wildlife. In marked contrast, fish and game were still plentiful in the Beaver River region.

So, in May 1896 Rapalje boarded an eastbound train in Buffalo. At Rochester, Leander Shaw and his friend Chester Wilcox joined Rapalje on the train. At Utica they met the three Elmira members of their fishing party and they all boarded a northbound train on the Adirondack branch of the New York Central.[4] It was late in the day by the time they reached Beaver River Station. Chet Elliott probably met the train with his horses and wagon. It was only a short ride to Elliott's Camp where they were staying.[5] At Elliott's they met their guide, James H. "Jimmy" Wilder. They may not have known it then, but that day the Rap-Shaw Club was born.

The name Rap-Shaw was most likely coined by Wilder. It was common back in those days for the guide to give a group of sportsmen under his direction a nickname.[6] This would usually be the name of the person who organized the trip and paid the deposit, or it could be the name of the location where the sportsmen lived. Since Rapalje and his friend Shaw had arranged for Jimmy Wilder to be their guide, it is likely that Wilder nicknamed their group the "Rap-Shaw party" by combining the last names of the two most prominent organizers. In time the name stuck.[7]

### The Founders

It is impossible to be sure of the identity of all the founding members of the Rap-Shaw Club. Existing records clearly show that the two primary organizers were Rapalje and Shaw. Rapalje owned a Buffalo fire prevention-equipment company and Shaw was the funeral director in Fairport, just outside Rochester.

Over the next five years, other sportsmen from the Buffalo, Elmira, and Rochester areas joined the original group on their trips to the Beaver River country. From Elmira there was Adam Mander, a prosperous brewer; John Deister, a grocer; and Robert Walker, a master plumber. Rapalje's business partner, Bert H. Wattles, was an early joiner. Another was Syracuse businessman Charles H. Pierce.[8] Erastus C. Knight, a prominent Buffalo politician, was another.

The diversity of the founders' professions is striking. The club was founded by men who sold fire prevention equipment, an undertaker, a master plumber, a lawyer, a dry-goods store owner, a grocer, a brewer, and a politician who lived in three different cities in central and western New York. What they all had in common was a strong desire to camp, hunt, and fish in the Beaver River country and the fact that they employed Jimmy Wilder as their guide.

### First Trips: 1896 and 1897

In the spring of 1896, Rapalje and his party used the Elliott Camp as their headquarters.[9] For a few days they tried their luck at nearby Loon and Big Burnt lakes but found the fishing unsatisfactory. Wilder suggested they go fifteen miles farther back in the woods along the Red Horse Trail to Big Crooked Lake, where he had built an open camp.[10]

51. Open camp, Big Crooked Lake, Jimmy Wilder at the table, uncredited photograph, Rap-Shaw Photo Album image 2-120. Courtesy of the Rap-Shaw Club, Inc.

They took his advice and the next day, in five hours of nonstop fishing at Big Crooked Lake, the six sportsmen caught 163 brook trout weighing a total of 165 pounds. They packed the fish in wet moss to keep them as fresh as possible. The following day the party returned to Elliott's carrying their prize. They managed to get a photographer to document their catch because they knew their friends back home would not otherwise believe their story. When spread out for display, the fish covered a board eleven feet long and two and a half feet wide as well as the top of a big dry goods box.

After the spectacular success of the first fishing trip, Rapalje, Shaw, and friends returned in the fall of 1896 for deer hunting. That trip must have also been a success because Rapalje and eight other founding club members returned for the 1897 spring fishing season. By this time the founders had made an arrangement with Jimmy Wilder. They agreed to hire Wilder as their guide for both spring fishing and fall hunting for the foreseeable future. In return, Wilder agreed to build the group a cabin in the vicinity of the Red Horse Trail for their exclusive use. Rapalje's notes suggest that in the spring of 1897 this cabin was already under construction on the shore of nearby Beaver Dam Pond.

### Beaver Dam Pond Cabins: 1897–1901

The first cabin Jimmy Wilder built for the Rap-Shaw party was a classic one-room affair with a sleeping loft, sided with small vertical logs. This "stockade style" cabin was common at the time. Judging from the earliest photographs of this camp in the Rap-Shaw archive, it was first used during the fall hunting season of 1897. By 1900 this camp was being heavily used by the Rap-Shaw party, so Wilder built a second cabin nearby. Wilder also had an older guide's cabin nearby along the trail from Witchhopple Lake.

An important technicality of the Beaver Dam Pond camp was its location inside the boundaries of Dr. Webb's private Nehasane Preserve. Wilder must have known he was building on Webb's land and chosen the Beaver Dam Pond location in part because it was not

52. Bert Wattles at rear of the first Rap-Shaw Club cabin at Beaver Dam Pond, 1897, uncredited photograph, Rap-Shaw Photo Album image 1-289. Courtesy of the Rap-Shaw Club, Inc.

directly on any established trail and not much visited. There is no evidence Wilder ever requested permission from Nehasane to build the Rap-Shaw camp. Squatting on private and state land was fairly common for guides of this time. From the early days of the nineteenth century, guides had built temporary camps all over the Beaver River region and encountered little or no objection from the absentee landowners.[11]

By 1901, times had changed. Perhaps triggered by the building of the second cabin, perhaps by the ever-increasing number of Rap-Shaw members hunting and fishing on its private property, Nehasane delivered an eviction notice. Jimmy Wilder was ordered to dismantle or destroy his camp by the end of the year. The nascent Rap-Shaw Club had reached its first major challenge.

## Witchhopple Lake Camp: 1902–16

When Nehasane evicted Wilder and the Rap-Shaw camp from Beaver Dam Pond, the members of the club had to assess their resources and their desire to continue to hunt and fish in the Beaver River country. By March 1901 they had reached a decision. They would relocate the camp onto state-owned Forest Preserve land at the foot of nearby Witchhopple Lake.

Viewed from our historical perspective, this decision seems questionable. From their perspective, it must have seemed eminently reasonable. Their first priority was to stay in the area they knew and loved. The only way to do this legally would have been to acquire some of the only available private land near Beaver River Station. But what if the state granted them permission to have their camp on state land? This seemed like a real possibility since there were already quite a few private camps on state land. (The camps on the Forest Preserve are discussed in chapter 10.)

In order to put forward the best possible case for allowing the camp onto state land, they decided to formally incorporate as a sportsmen's club. They must have reasoned that if the state knew the club was comprised of prosperous businessmen and community leaders from around upstate, they would be more likely to look favorably on their request. Incorporation papers were filed on March 4, 1901, formally creating the Rap-Shaw Fishing Club.[12] Rapalje was elected president of the board and Shaw was elected vice president.[13]

As soon as the Rap-Shaw Club was incorporated, Rapalje secured an interview in Watertown with DeWitt Middleton, a commissioner of the Forest, Fish and Game Commission. Jimmy Wilder accompanied Rapalje to the meeting. After they stated their case, Middleton told them he was unable to grant the club permission for a camp on the Forest Preserve, but if the club moved onto state land they did so at their own risk. That was good enough for the founders.[14] Over the next winter both cabins from the Wilder camp at Beaver Dam Pond were moved to Witchhopple Lake. The two cabins were combined and expanded to make one larger clubhouse. The relocated camp was ready to open for the 1902 fishing season.

The site at Witchhopple Lake was an immediate hit with club members. It was somewhat closer and easier to reach, being directly on the Red Horse Trail. Witchhopple Lake was beautiful and had good boating. The area's trails, summits, and lakes were more easily reached from the new campsite.

Shortly after the relocation, some members began to make arrangements to visit the camp during the summer season, not for fishing or hunting but simply to vacation. During the summer of 1903, the club recorded its first women visitors. Over the next few years Jimmy Wilder added three small cabins with tarpaper sides to accommodate families.

53. No. 5 Wilders Camp, Witchhopple Lake, uncredited photo postcard, Rap-Shaw Photo Album image 1-15. Courtesy of the Rap-Shaw Club, Inc.

At the beginning of the 1906 season, the club purchased the buildings from Wilder. Jimmy Wilder and his wife, Evelyn, were hired as the club's first stewards.[15] The Wilders remained the club's stewards for ten more years.

In the fall of 1915, the Conservation Commission finally decided the time had come to evict the squatters from the Forest Preserve lands throughout the Adirondacks. All the camps along the Red Horse Trail, including the Rap-Shaw Club, were served with legal notices that they must immediately remove their buildings or have them destroyed.[16]

At its meeting on April 4, 1916, the board decided it would move the camp back to Beaver Dam Pond on land leased from Nehasane Park. At that same meeting John P. Rapalje was reelected club president; however, he died five weeks later on May 10, 1916. Shaw had died in March 1911. On July 10, 1916, Jimmy and Evelyn Wilder tendered their resignations as club stewards effective at the end of October.[17] It was the end of an era, and time for a new beginning.

54. Veranda of Rap-Shaw Fishing Club, Witchhopple Lake in the Adirondacks, uncredited photo postcard, Rap-Shaw Photo Album image 2-20. Courtesy of the Rap-Shaw Club, Inc.

## Beaver Dam Pond Camp: 1917–39

Negotiating a lease of land at Beaver Dam Pond proved to be difficult. The relationship between the Rap-Shaw Club and Dr. Webb's Nehasane Park Association was not an easy one. No doubt Dr. Webb was still a bit wary because the club's first cabins had been built on Nehasane's private property without his permission. In the intervening years, however, the relationship had mellowed quite a bit. Nehasane's game protectors knew that Rap-Shaw members were careful not to trespass on Nehasane property to hunt or fish. Club members took pride in being known as responsible sportsmen. They maintained the trails in their domain. They placed boats on the lakes for anyone to use. They aided with the enforcement of fish and game laws against poaching.

Negotiations were concluded at the Rap-Shaw Board meeting on April 3, 1916. The draft lease was quite one-sided. It contained numerous restrictions on usage, but the Rap-Shaw Board was not in position to bargain. Moving back to Beaver Dam Pond was pretty much their only viable option. In the end, the club agreed to lease ten acres at the old club campsite on the west end of Beaver Dam Pond for an annual rent of $300, or about $6,700 in today's dollars. The lease had a term of five years and was renewable.

Nehasane Park was wary about opening its doors to outsiders. The lease limited access to no more than forty different club members in any year. This was significant because in 1916 the club had seventy-nine members.[18] Furthermore, each member of the club was permitted to invite only one guest a year and no more than twenty-five persons, including members and guests, were permitted to use the camp at any one time. The club had to annually submit copies of their guest registers to Nehasane for inspection.[19]

Massive forest fires in 1903 and 1908 burned over six hundred thousand acres in the Adirondacks. The most sensational of the 1908 fires destroyed the village of Long Lake West (now called Sabattis) and charred everything along the railroad tracks all the way to Nehasane Park at Lake Lila. Given this close call, preventing forest fires was a top priority for Nehasane. The lease required the club maintain specific firefighting equipment, required members of the club to report and fight fires on their territory, and required that any member found to be careless with fire be immediately expelled.[20]

As soon as the lease was finalized, the board made plans to relocate. Over the winter all the buildings were skidded about a mile east over frozen Witchhopple Lake and the surrounding marsh using rollers and teams of horses. They again enlarged the clubhouse by annexing a club member's cabin and turning it into a comfortable living room with a fireplace.[21] By the spring of 1917, the new camp was ready.

Every time the lease came up for renewal over the next twenty years, the Rap-Shaw Board made efforts to purchase the site. Even though these efforts were always unsuccessful, it is easy to understand why club members wanted to own it. Every year, the club spent considerable money improving the camp and its fittings. Most members were small business owners who quite naturally were not enthusiastic

LIVING ROOM AT THE
RAP-SHAW CLUB HOUSE

55. The living room at the Rap-Shaw clubhouse at Beaver Dam Pond, uncredited photo postcard, Rap-Shaw Photo Album image 2-53. Courtesy of the Rap-Shaw Club, Inc.

about spending money to develop leased property. The club had been displaced twice before. They were only too aware that Nehasane Preserve could evict them again if circumstances changed.

During the fall 1917 hunting season, Jimmy and Evelyn Wilder returned from their brief retirement to operate the camp. Perhaps this is when the Wilders suggested the board consider hiring their daughter and son-in-law as the next stewards. The board saw wisdom in that idea and hired Herbert and Anna Nye. This decision should go down as one of the best ever made by the Rap-Shaw Board. Herbie and Anna Nye went on to serve the club as stewards continuously until 1958, a total of forty years.

### The Choice: Exclusive or Open to All?

In general, two types of sportsmen were drawn to join Rap-Shaw during the 1910s. Most members were modestly well-off and owned small businesses. A smaller but significant group was wealthier and more politically well-connected. This second group wanted to transform Rap-Shaw into a more exclusive club along the lines of the nearby Beaver River Club.

This tension came to a head at a contentious annual meeting held on December 6, 1920, at the Statler Hotel in Buffalo. A group of wealthy board members put forward a proposal to raise annual dues substantially, thereby forcing out the less prosperous members. Attorneys for each side hotly contested the validity of each proxy ballot. When the dust cleared, the dues increase was soundly defeated. Three members who pledged to keep the club modest and affordable were elected to the board. Over the next few months those who wanted to belong to a more exclusive club resigned. Ever since that decision, the club has dedicated itself to remaining affordable.

### Fish Stocking by Airplane

In the fall of 1923, legendary member D. E. Hartnett[22] wrote a letter to the Rap-Shaw Board suggesting that the club stock fish in the surrounding lakes and ponds. Instead of stocking fish themselves that year, the club decided to write the Conservation Department to see if they would stock Walker, Clear and Little Rock Lakes for summer fishing.[23]

The main obstacle to effective stocking of these remote lakes was finding a practical way to transport heavy cans of fish from the hatchery at Old Forge to the waters near the club. Following a number of years of unsuccessful pleas to the Conservation Department, the club decided to proceed on its own. At the annual meeting in December 1931, Hartnett reported that the solution to the fish transportation problem was to fly the fish in by floatplane.[24] The board allocated $150 to cover this cost. Hartnett arranged for early Adirondack aviator Merrill Phoenix to do the job.[25]

The next August, Phoenix's plane called at the state fish hatchery at Old Forge and received as many as twenty cans of fingerling trout at a time. Club members met the plane and stood in the cold water up to their hips to temper the fingerlings before releasing them. Phoenix

56. Fish stocking on Witchhopple Lake in 1932, pilot Merrill Phoenix and D. E. Hartnett on the pontoon, uncredited photograph, Rap-Shaw Photo Album image 1-152. Courtesy of the Rap-Shaw Club, Inc.

made seven flights that first year planting fish in lakes favored by club fishermen, including Big Crooked, Witchhopple, Willie, Walker and Clear Lakes. Hartnett was on the plane for several of the trips. Legend has it that when flying over the camps at Beaver River Station Hartnett dropped notes and dollar bills to the kids below in empty tomato cans.[26]

Word spread quickly that the club was the first to ever successfully use an airplane for fish stocking. Articles praising the idea appeared in newspapers throughout the state and in national sporting magazines.

Buoyed by their success, Hartnett and the fish committee continued to stock fish by floatplane annually through 1938.[27] The cost kept incrementally rising, and in 1935 the board sharply reduced the budget of the fish committee. It was, after all, the heart of the Depression, and the club needed to pinch every penny. Finally, in the late 1930s the Conservation Department started to use airplanes for fish stocking in remote waters throughout the Adirondacks, but instead of landing floatplanes, they simply dropped fingerling fish from the air.

## Williams Island Camp: 1939 to the Present

A catastrophic event sometime early in 1938 precipitated the club's final move. No one knows exactly how or when it happened. Very early that spring two local teenage boys went exploring up the Red Horse Trail.[28] According to former DEC ranger Terry Perkins, these boys were the first to discover that the Rap-Shaw Clubhouse at Beaver Dam Pond had burned.[29] Further inspection revealed the main clubhouse and nearby woodshed were completely destroyed. The three club cabins, the generator shed, and the toolshed were undamaged.

As the board debated rebuilding, they learned that Nehasane Park was now willing to sell the club 960 acres immediately surrounding Beaver Dam Pond for $25 per acre or a total of $24,000, about $421,000 in today's dollars. Insurance proceeds on the loss of the Beaver Dam clubhouse were $3,000. While this would cover the expense of building a new clubhouse, the club members did not collectively have adequate financial resources to buy the land at Webb's asking price. Accordingly, the board decided not to accept the Webb proposal.

President John Scopes favored a different plan. Herbie Nye had made him aware that an existing camp called the Stillwater Club[30] had recently come up for sale. It was located on two islands in the Stillwater Reservoir quite near the Stillwater boat landing at the west end of the reservoir. This camp, with all existing buildings and fittings, could be purchased for the amount owed on the mortgages and back taxes. The total cost was estimated to be about six thousand dollars. After an inspection tour, the board saw the wisdom of relocating to the island camp. The purchase process was complicated. The club eventually obtained clear title following a foreclosure sale on June 27, 1940.[31]

The camp the club bought on Williams Island was composed entirely of salvaged buildings and materials from the Beaver River Club. The main camp building was the relocated Camp Wild-a-While. Several of the ancillary buildings, such as the boathouse and icehouse, had also been moved intact. The dining hall and kitchen were built out of salvaged materials, as were two duplex sleeping cabins. An original guide's camp from the Beaver River Club sat at the top of the much smaller Chicken Island across from the dining hall.[32] The cabins were fully furnished and had indoor plumbing.

### The Sportsmen's Club Becomes a Family Summer Camp

The Rap-Shaw Club took possession of the Williams Island camp in the fall of 1939 while purchase negotiations proceeded. Such equipment as could be salvaged from the camp at Beaver Dam Pond was moved to the island, as were the club's best boats. A full contingent of members signed up to use the new camp during the November deer season.

Even though the club's membership continued to hover in the neighborhood of one hundred throughout the 1940s, economic conditions during the Second World War caused camp usage to decline. By 1949 the treasurer bemoaned the fact that even with ninety-five dues-paying members, on average each member only used the club three days per year. Low usage resulted in significant annual operating losses. In the 1949 season alone the club lost more than $1,500.[33] Many years the club had to borrow money to meet expenses. The trend continued through the 1950s. Some years the club took out bank loans to make up for the deficit; in other years special assessments were levied on members in addition to regular dues.[34]

The board understood that during the war years money was tight. During the 1940s, annual dues were kept low so no one was forced out because of inability to pay. In an attempt to solve the problem permanently, the board gradually introduced a number of financial measures to increase revenue, realizing that achieving lasting financial stability depended on finding ways to increase usage of the club.

They knew camp usage was strong during early spring fishing. Summer usage by families was also strong through the months of July and August, but few members used the club during deer hunting season. In the fall of 1955, no one signed up for deer hunting and the

57. Uri French (left) and John Scopes (right) at Beaver Dam Pond, about 1935, uncredited photograph, Rap-Shaw Photo Album image 1-166. Courtesy of the Rap-Shaw Club, Inc.

club closed during November for the first time. In 1958, the board formed a committee to try to find a way to make fall hunting economically self-sustaining, but after a year of study it reported there was little likelihood that hunting could ever be resumed.

Fearing that newer members might not share the fanatical interest the older members had in fishing, two former presidents from Elmira, Uri French (president 1945–50) and John Scopes (president 1932–45) initiated the club's first fishing derby in 1950.[35] They donated suitably impressive trophies. One was to be awarded for the single heaviest native trout taken during the season and one was to be awarded for the largest single day's catch of native trout by weight.

At the end of the season an article titled, "Trophies Awarded! Fishermen, Hide Your Heads," appeared in the *Rap-Shaw Review*. The author set the scene:

> We have some excellent fishermen. Some of these men have been fishing for over 50 years. Many of these men are experts with a fly rod, others excel at trolling. Most of these men have been coming to the Club for over 10 years and some even 20 and 30. The majority of them know the best streams and holes and how and where to get the best fishing. Most of our men did fish hard, and had

there been a trophy for effort, it would have been hard to decide the winner.[36]

The upshot, of course, was that none of the club's male members won either trophy that first year. The French trophy for the heaviest fish was awarded to Mrs. Charles Darymple and the Scopes trophy for the best day's catch was awarded to Helen (Mrs. Henry) Murphy.[37] The fishing derby, now dubbed the Black Fly Fishing Derby, continues to this day.

With the future of fishing secure and hunting coming to an end, the club turned its attention to improving facilities to attract better attendance by families during the summer season. The dining room was renovated and each of the cabins repaired. A shuffleboard court was built next to the horseshoe pits. An electric cable was strung across the water from the mainland and all the cabins wired. Three electric refrigerators and a freezer were purchased for the dining hall. Once the icehouse was no longer needed for its original purpose, it was converted to a shower house, and a bathroom with shower was added to Chicken Island camp. These improvements paid off by bringing more families to camp, many staying for a week or more. This trend improved the club's financial condition, but also fundamentally altered the camping experience for members.

The story of the *Big Boat* is emblematic of this change.[38] The *Big* was one of the boats moved from Beaver Dam to Williams Island. Built in 1925 by club members in Joe Gorthy's shop in Buffalo, then sent to Beaver River Station by rail, it was fashioned along the lines of a lifeboat from the Great Lakes steamers. A favorite all-day family camp activity during the 1950s was to take a group on a Big Boat ride to Beaver River Station.[39]

Annie [Nye] would pack a hamper with wieners, buns, pickles, olives, coffee and one of her delicious soft gingerbread cakes (and milk for the little ones) plus dishes and cooking equipment and off we would go with Herbie to guide us safely through the stump-filled waters. If the Flow was low enough, we would find a sandy beach

58. The *Big Boat* fully loaded, about 1950, uncredited photograph, Rap-Shaw Photo Album image 1-171. Courtesy of the Rap-Shaw Club, Inc.

where we would land, have a swim then cook our lunch. The boat would hold 10 adults and many more little ones under foot. Then we would poke around in the back bays and inlets sometimes going into Trout Pond or Big Burnt, but eventually landing at Grassy Point where we could walk the mile up the road to Beaver River station to watch the train come in!

By the end of the 1950s, the days of the old club were coming to an end. Almost all of the members who knew the club at Witchhopple and Beaver Dam were gone. Even though they knew it would eventually happen, in 1957 the members expressed dismay when Herbie and Annie Nye announced their retirement after serving the club faithfully for forty seasons. As if to mark the end of an era, on February 2, 1958, Jimmy Wilder, who had been the soul of the club since 1896, died at the age of eighty-seven.

### The Rap-Shaw Club Today

By the time the Nyes retired, the Rap-Shaw Club had been transformed from the hunting and fishing camp of the Witchhopple and

Beaver Dam days to a family-oriented summer camp. Fishing and boating remained mainstays but hunting never resumed after 1954. In the old days, the club was open only during the early spring fishing season and the late fall deer hunting season. Now the club is fully booked between July 4 and Labor Day but only lightly used in May, June, and September. In its early days the club regularly had upward of one hundred members, all men. Now the club is comprised of sixty-five families and about half of the members of the board of directors are women.

Many things have not changed. As in the old days, accommodations are simple and rustic. Three simple meals a day are served family style in the dining hall; the menu changes daily. The loud clanging of an old train bell summons campers to meals. Children are responsible for busing the tables.

Activities can be as simple as reading a book in an Adirondack chair or rocking quietly in a fishing boat. Canoeing, kayaking, and paddleboarding are popular. Children spend their time on the natural sand beach, swimming, boating, or playing games. There are several opportunities for hiking nearby. On many evenings there is a campfire with stories, singing, and making s'mores.[40]

The traditions of the Rap-Shaw Club are strong. It is not unusual to find groups at camp made up of three or even four generations. New members are welcomed as space permits. Everyone agrees that the club is a place where everyday concerns are left behind. The power of the forest, the water, and the haunting call of the loon always produce a peaceful state of mind not easily found elsewhere.

# Part Five

# Settlement at Stillwater

59. The Beaver River Inn / Old Homestead, undated photo postcard by Henry M. Beach with revised caption. Collection of the author.

# 13

# Stillwater Hotels

There have been accommodations of some sort at Stillwater ever since 1845, when hermit Jimmy O'Kane started to take in travelers at the cabin he commandeered from the road builders next to the Twitchell Creek bridge. O'Kane's cabin was followed by the Wardwell pioneer homestead. The Dunbar Hotel replaced Wardwell's. Dunbar's gave way to the elegant clubhouse of the Beaver River Club.

The 1925 dam flooded the area where all of these early accommodations once stood. The current Stillwater Hotel is the sole surviving descendant of this line of historic hostelries. Its story begins in 1906 when the Old Homestead Hotel opened to the public.

### Churchill's Old Homestead: May 1906–October 1910

As discussed in chapters 9 and 10, sporting tourism became the backbone of the economy of the Beaver River country soon after the passenger railroad started to run in late 1892. For the next decade or so, the influx of sportsmen was accommodated at a handful of small hotels near Beaver River Station, at the Rap-Shaw and the Beaver River Clubs, and at the elegant original Norridgewock Hotel. All of these establishments flourished. The tide of tourists grew steadily and showed no sign of abating.

The Beaver River Club hired H. C. (Henry Charles) Churchill at the beginning of 1902 to replace Pop Bullock, who resigned to run his own Grassy Point Inn. The Churchill family was from Binghamton, New York. In 1902, Henry was forty-five. His wife, Anna Mayo Churchill, was forty. They had three young daughters: Alice, fourteen;

(Anna) Louise, ten; and Lena, seven. During the hunting and fishing seasons while their parents were living at the Beaver River Club, the girls went to school in Lyons Falls, where they boarded with a family. They lived in Binghamton the rest of the year.[1]

H. C. Churchill was a good hotel manager. His first employment in the Beaver River area appears to have been in 1901 when he served as manager of Stanton's Adirondack Camp.[2] Churchill next served as the Beaver River Club manager from June 1902 until October 1905. One of Churchill's duties at the Beaver River Club was to transport club members and guests from the train at Beaver River Station. The first leg of the journey was covered in Pop Bullock's buckboard from the station to Grassy Point on the Beaver River. The rest of the trip was by boat about eight miles down the Beaver River Flow to Stillwater. To make the river trip more comfortable, Churchill ordered a twenty-five-foot steam launch from boat builder D. H. Tuttle of Canastota, New York. Churchill named this boat *Alice* after his eldest daughter.[3]

H. C. Churchill was a smart businessman. He knew the Beaver River Club was doing well financially. When he took over as manager

60. The steamer *Alice* docked at the Old Homestead, uncredited photograph from the Churchill-Shaver Album. Courtesy of Jim and Carol Fox.

in 1902, the club had just completed a fine new clubhouse that cost ten thousand dollars. Lots were being sold as prime real estate. Wealthy families from all over Central New York were building elegant new camps. Churchill knew there was a need for more tourist accommodations at the west end of the Flow. Perhaps encouraged by the success of Pop Bullock's Grassy Point Inn, Churchill resigned as manager of the Beaver River Club at the end of the 1905 season and built his own fine hotel.

That hotel, named the Old Homestead, opened in the spring of 1906 near the west end of the first bridge to Dunbar Island. Its advertising brochure claimed visitors could expect "good health, rest, good water, plenty to eat, and a general good time." The hotel had plastered walls. The windows were screened against insects. Wide porches surrounded the building on both levels. The reception area was furnished with rustic Adirondack furniture and a large fireplace. The Churchill family grew their own fresh vegetables, had a cow for milk, and kept

61. Front view of the Old Homestead, uncredited photograph from the Churchill-Shaver Album. Courtesy of Jim and Carol Fox.

Reception Room, Old Homestead, Beaver River, N. Y.    Souvenir Card Co.
Ellisburg, N. Y.

62. Reception room of the Old Homestead, uncredited photo postcard from the Churchill-Shaver Album. Courtesy of Jim and Carol Fox.

chickens for eggs. Canoes and rowboats of all sizes were provided to guests at no extra cost.

The first entry in the Old Homestead's guest register was on May 5, 1906. Review of that guest register shows the new hotel quickly became a success.[4] Due to its proximity to the Beaver River Club and its fine amenities, it attracted a distinguished clientele, such as noted Arts and Crafts furniture makers J. G., Leopold, and Charles Stickley.[5] During Christmas of 1908, the Old Homestead entertained fifteen guests from New York, Texas, Maryland, Connecticut, Pennsylvania, and the Netherlands.

### Young's Beaver River Inn:
### October 1910–November 1924

Well-known local guide Harlow C. Young replaced Churchill as manager at the Beaver River Club at the beginning of 1906. By that time, he had been guiding sporting tourists through the Beaver River country for ten years or more. Harlow was born on February 21, 1865. He grew up on the east side of the Black River in the Lewis County town of Watson on the edge of the Beaver River wilderness. He married a neighbor, Minnie J. Schmidlin, on January 6, 1892. Minnie was born on May 19, 1872. Minnie's father was Joseph W. Schmidlin and her mother was Harriet Wilder.[6]

There were few settlers in Watson in those days so it should not come as a surprise that many families were related by marriage. It is interesting, however, that three of the people responsible for important developments along the upper Beaver River, Harlow Young, Jimmy Wilder and Elmer Wilder, were all first cousins.[7]

After Harlow and Minnie married, they settled in Crystaldale, a small community along the Number Four Road. The Wilder family lived nearby. When the railroad started carrying passengers to Beaver River Station in 1892, Harlow Young and Jimmy Wilder, both recently married young men, decided to supplement their income by becoming outdoors guides. By 1897 they had joined forces to construct a semipermanent open camp at Witchhopple Lake along the Red Horse Trail to be used during the fishing and hunting seasons.[8]

Guiding part-time and farming full-time was a hard and unpredictable way to earn a living. By 1900, Harlow Young had acquired a job as a brakeman on the railroad. For a few years he and Minnie lived in Utica so he could be near the New York Central mainline.[9] Minnie's father had died in 1896, but her mother still lived in Watson, so there was probably some pressure for the Young family to return to the North Country. Sometime before 1902 Harlow had saved enough money to build a fairly large house in Crystaldale and open the downstairs as a general store.[10] As the only storekeeper, he was also appointed Crystaldale postmaster in 1902.[11]

Harlow was experienced both as a guide and as a businessman so, in 1906 when the manager's job at the Beaver River Club opened up, he was a natural choice. Harlow hired a clerk to run the store in

Crystaldale.[12] He and Minnie moved to the Beaver River Clubhouse for the tourist season that ran from May to October.[13]

During his time at the Beaver River Club, Harlow Young became friends with Henry M. Beach, the well-known Lowville photographer.[14] Beach visited the Beaver River region frequently. He sold racks of custom real picture postcards to the Beaver River Club, the Old Homestead, and the Norridgewock Hotel at Beaver River Station. As noted in chapter 10, Henry's brother, Louis Beach, managed the Norridgewock from about 1908 until the early 1920s. Most of the surviving photographs of the Beaver River Club and the neighboring hotels and camps were made or published by Henry Beach.[15]

Harlow was accustomed to being an independent businessman. He also seems to have had the gift of foresight. Right next door to the Beaver River Club, the Old Homestead Hotel was attracting distinguished guests and making money. The rates there were significantly lower than those the directors of the Beaver River Club needed to charge to service their debt. Harlow saw that the business model of the Old Homestead was clearly superior. It was family-run with low overhead. Harlow knew the local guides, knew the hotel business, and was even experienced in the advertising end of things. On October 20, 1910, he resigned as manager of the Beaver River Club and bought the Old Homestead. He renamed it the Beaver River Inn.[16]

Young made few changes to the building or the operations. The guest registers from the years he and Minnie operated the hotel show that he maintained a steady clientele. For example, the *Lowville Journal and Republican* reported on August 21, 1913, that twenty guests were staying at the Beaver River Inn. Most guests stayed a week or more. Although the hotel was usually closed in the winter, Minnie Young managed to successfully host a surprise fiftieth birthday party for her husband in February 1915. The party included a "straw ride" for their neighbors from Crystaldale seventeen miles to the Beaver River Inn, where an elaborate birthday dinner was held.[17]

By 1919, landowners all along the upper Beaver River knew that the state intended to significantly enlarge the dam at Stillwater.[18] Even though the details had not yet been fixed, Harlow Young made

63. Portrait of Harlow Young in 1941, uncredited photograph. Courtesy of Dennis Buckley.

plans to adapt. First, he purchased a house on Sharp Street in Lowville so he and Minnie would have a place to live if the Beaver River Inn was flooded.[19] In 1921, when the Black River Regulating District released detailed maps showing the projected new high-water line and listing the properties to be flooded, the Youngs knew for certain that the Beaver River Inn would not be spared. On August 30, 1923, the Youngs sold the land under the Beaver River Inn to the state of New York.[20] They continued to operate the inn until November 1924, and then closed the doors for good.

### The Stillwater Hotel: 1925 to the Present

Harlow and Minnie Young did not intend to retire from the hotel business just yet. The state had purchased their land but not their buildings. As soon as the hotel closed, they dismantled the Beaver River Inn and salvaged what they could. Fixtures like windows, doors, stairs, finished lumber, fittings, plumbing, and so on were stripped from the hotel and moved to a large lot the Youngs purchased on nearby higher ground. They used some of this material to build a new, smaller hotel. Some of the material was used to build the Youngs' new camp, high on a hill behind the hotel.[21]

By the summer of 1925, the reincarnated Beaver River Inn opened for business. The new hotel was "somewhat smaller but more pretentious" than the original.[22] During the next few years, as the Stillwater

64. Beaver River Inn, D. J. Purcell, Ppr., P.O. Number Four, New York, undated
photo postcard by Henry M. Beach. Collection of the author.

Reservoir gradually gained a reputation as a fine place for boating and
fishing, the established clientele kept the Youngs busy and prosperous.
At the end of the 1927 season, they decided to retire. Minnie was fifty-
five, Harlow sixty-two. They sold the hotel to Douglas J. Purcell of
Lowville[23] and moved permanently to their house in Lowville.

In May 1928 the Purcell family, including D. J. Purcell, his wife
Catherine "Kate" Yousey, and their youngest son Robert J., took over.
For a time, the Purcells' hotel continued to be known as the Beaver
River Inn. By the late 1920s, however, a small vacation community,
commonly referred to as Stillwater, had grown up at the west end of
the Stillwater Reservoir where the road from Lowville ended. The
Purcells wanted to be sure customers did not mistakenly think their
hotel was located near the railroad station in the settlement of Beaver
River at the other end of the reservoir. To avoid any confusion about
location, the Purcells changed the name to the Stillwater Hotel. It has
been known by that name ever since.

Douglas Purcell died of a stroke in May 1938.[24] Kate Purcell continued to operate the hotel with the assistance of her son Robert and his wife Catherine Beaton.[25] The Purcell family ran the hotel for twelve more years, until April 1950.

Minnie and Harlow Young both died in the fall of 1943.[26] They had no children. Pearl Smith, a niece who had lived with them in Lowville for a number of years, inherited their estate. Apparently, at the time of his death Harlow Young still held the Purcells' mortgage on the Stillwater Hotel. For some unknown reason, by April 1950 the Purcells were no longer able to operate the hotel. Pearl

R.J.PURCELL. 3 BROOK TROUT
4¾ AND 3 AND 2 POUNDS
CAUGHT IN STILLWATER RESERVOIR
MAY 31,1934

65. Promotional postcard of Robert J. Purcell, uncredited photo postcard. Courtesy of Timothy Mayers.

Smith foreclosed and took back the property. She had no intention of running the hotel herself and looked for a new buyer. During that summer she sold the Stillwater Hotel to Emmett and Marge Hill.

Before buying the Stillwater Hotel, Emmett Hill worked as a forest ranger based in Glenfield in the Black River valley.[27] In those days forest rangers were politically appointed. When he decided to buy the Stillwater Hotel, Hill wanted to keep working as a ranger, so he arranged for his political friends to subdivide the jurisdiction of Ranger Bill Marleau of Big Moose Station.

The rationale given for this division was connected to the fire tower on Stillwater Mountain. The fire observer had to report to the supervising ranger by telephone several times a day. The Stillwater tower's telephone line ran from the fire tower to Marleau's ranger headquarters at Big Moose Station.[28] Until 1955 there was no road from Big Moose Station to Stillwater. In order to check in with the fire observer in person, Marleau would have to hike for miles cross-country or take the train to Beaver River Station and then a boat back down the reservoir to the trail to Stillwater Mountain. Either trip took quite a bit of time. A round trip was an all-day affair. Having a ranger at Stillwater made trips to the fire tower faster and easier.

Although Marleau originally resented Hill considerably for taking away some of his territory, they eventually learned to get along and often did projects together. For example, Bill Marleau told former Ranger Terry Perkins about a time when Emmett took his very young son Billy along on a joint ranger mission to repair a lean-to on the Red Horse Trail. Billy apparently caused a commotion and proved a distraction. Emmett decided to get him out of the way by hanging him by his belt from a spike driven into a tree nearby. There Billy hung, kicking and screaming, until the job was complete.

Emmett had a reputation as a heavy drinker. His main renovation to the hotel was the addition of the current barroom. Emmett used the bar as his ranger office while his wife, Marge, managed the hotel and did the cooking. Eventually, complaints about the use of a barroom as a ranger station reached Albany. As a result, the Conservation Department decided that a separate ranger office should be built at Stillwater. The ranger's cabin that still stands near the landing was built during 1966. Hill hired his son-in-law, Bob Griswold, to build the cabin.

Emmett Hill did not intend to use the new cabin as his office. Instead, he left it mostly unfinished and retired. The next ranger, Bill Richardson, was the first to briefly occupy it. The cabin was still unfinished when the next ranger, Terry Perkins, moved to Stillwater later in 1967. Terry and his wife, Diane, moved into the cabin, finished its construction, and lived there until Terry retired in 1998.

Emmett Hill, always a heavy smoker, died of lung cancer in 1967. Marge Hill continued to operate the hotel until 1972.

Two developments that would prove to be consequential occurred while the Hills owned the hotel. For many years, visitors to Stillwater could arrive by train at Beaver River Station or by automobile by traveling the long dirt road from Lowville. Beginning in the 1920s, the road was slowly improved, and road traffic increased.[29] After the Second World War, the private automobile became the preferred mode of tourist transportation. Tourists tended to plan vacations at locations that could be reached on paved roads. Consequently, tourism flourished along the Fulton Chain. Stillwater was not connected by road to this growing flow of tourist dollars. Finally, in 1955 a dirt road was cut through from Big Moose to Stillwater.[30] It has never been paved. Although improved automobile access generally failed to greatly increase visitation to Stillwater, it did make living there more convenient.

The first snowmobile appeared in Stillwater in 1959. Winter visitation almost immediately took off. Pat Thompson remembered this transition vividly because her family was able to stop winter fur trapping and keep the Norridgewock Hotel open for the plentiful new business.[31] The Stillwater Hotel also soon became a regular stop for snowmobilers as winter became, and remains, a profitable tourist season.

A couple from western New York bought the Stillwater Hotel in 1972.[32] Dan Mahoney was a barber. He moved to Stillwater with his wife Sue and their two children, Jeff and Julie. Dan apparently was not a people person but was a good builder. Everybody loved Sue. She was outgoing, a good cook, and a good manager. People sometimes visited the hotel's restaurant specifically to sample Sue's sweet rolls. During the time they owned the hotel, the building was expanded substantially by encasing the original hotel in a new Swiss chalet–style building. The Mahoneys also built a small motel block behind the hotel to provide more modern accommodations. In 1988 they moved to Old Forge, where Sue opened a restaurant called the Muffin Patch while Dan worked as a carpenter with their son Jeff.

Marian and Walt Stroehmer from Rockland County, New York, just happened to be looking to buy a bed and breakfast in the Adirondacks in 1988 at the same time as the Mahoneys were ready to move to town. The Stroehmers wanted to find a place where Marian could

66. The Stillwater Hotel in 2021, photograph by Meredith Leonard.

pursue her hospitality skills and her love of fishing, canoeing, hiking, biking, and skiing. The Stillwater Hotel met their criteria.

Marian remembers that they fell in love with the beauty of the place as soon as they saw the reservoir stretching off into the distance. It snowed at Stillwater on the Fourth of July that year. Instead of being discouraged, Marian decided the snow was a sign that the hotel needed a gift shop where she could sell shivering campers a sweatshirt or two.

After Walt's untimely death, Marian continued to operate the hotel on her own. In 1994, Joe Romano became her husband and business partner. In order to improve the restaurant part of the business over the years, they expanded the kitchen, added a large deck overlooking the reservoir, and added a new dining area beyond the bar. The Romanos also updated the motel rooms and added a honeymoon suite by converting the former icehouse into a king guest room. They operate the hotel year-round. It continues to serve its traditional purpose as the de facto community center for Stillwater residents and visitors.

# 14

# The Stillwater Community

## The Origin of the Hamlet of Stillwater

There was no settlement at the spot where the old Carthage-to-Lake Champlain Road from Number Four emerged from the forest above the Beaver River rapids at Stillwater until the early years of the twentieth century.[1] Approaching the current site of the Stillwater community from the west about 1910, the first building a visitor would encounter was the Beaver River Inn. Just beyond the hotel, the road crossed a short bridge over Alder Creek to Dunbar Island.[2]

On the east side of the Alder Creek bridge, on the northwest end of Dunbar Island, sat the H. C. Churchill camp. The road skirted the next high hill (now Chicken Island) and then crossed the middle of a lower hill (now Williams Island). A few cottages lined the northeastern shore here. After descending this hill, the road crossed a short bridge over an inlet to reach the main section of the Beaver River Club. The road passed right next to the clubhouse, then downhill to the east side of the island where the road crossed the Twitchell Creek bridge to continue on to Beaver River Station.

When the 1901–2 concrete dam was under construction (see chapter 8), the state built a spur road to the dam. The state hired James C. "Jim" Dunbar to be the dam-keeper for the new dam. Jim Dunbar was the son of Joe and Mary Dunbar, former owners of the Dunbar Hotel. Jim and his wife, Clara Smith Dunbar, stayed on at Stillwater after his parents sold their hotel to the Beaver River Club in 1892. Jim and Clara bought a large piece of property in a level area along the

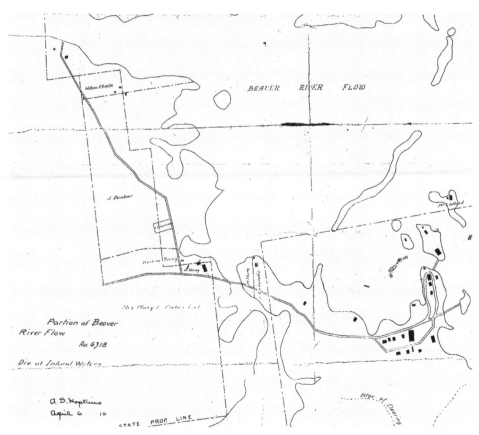

Map labels:
BEAVER RIVER FLOW

William A Smith

J. Dunbar

M. Kelland

Harlow Young

J. Young

Mrs Mary J Fisher Lot

Portion of Beaver
River Flow
Acc 6318

Div of Inland Waters

a. S. Hopkins
april 6    16

STATE PROP LINE

Below of Clearing

67. Detail from 1916 Hopkins map of a portion of the Beaver River Flow, Herkimer County Clerk's Office, Portion of Beaver River Flow, by A. S. Hopkins, Apr. 6, 1916.

68. Jim Dunbar in front of his farm with snowshoe hare, uncredited photograph from the Churchill-Shaver Album. Courtesy of Jim and Carol Fox.

road to the dam.[3] They built a substantial two-story farmhouse, barn, and outbuildings with a large subsistence garden and a pasture for the cows and horses.

Had the higher 1924 dam not been built, the Beaver River Club would have survived in some form and the Stillwater community probably would have developed on Dunbar Island along the western bank of Twitchell Creek. Because the 1924 dam was built, the Dunbar family, along with Harlow and Minnie Young, became the founders of the new Stillwater community.

*Dunbar Cottage Lots*

As the dam-keeper, Jim Dunbar was probably among the first to learn in 1919 about the state's plans for enlarging the dam. He must have immediately realized that about half of his property would be flooded and his farm destroyed. To adapt to this new reality, Jim and Lucy Dunbar[4] subdivided the property they owned that they knew would remain above the future high-water line. They created five small cottage lots along their future waterfront property. They retained a large lot behind the cottage lots for future development.

The cottage lots sold quickly. The Dunbars sold a lot on the north end of this parcel to I. S. Foster and Deat Harrington, who had been operating Camp Wiliwana at Wolf Creek Falls a few miles away up the Flow since 1915. They sold another lot to Jacob Zimmerman, who had a camp near the Dunbar farm. A third lot was purchased by H. C. Churchill, who relocated his cottage from Dunbar Island. As mentioned in the previous chapter, the relocated Churchill cottage, Forest Home, still stands. They sold a fourth lot to William and Frances Dancey of Rochester. The Danceys also purchased one of the oldest cottages from the Beaver River Club, had it carefully dismantled, and then reconstructed it on their future shoreline lot.[5] This camp, now known as the Dunbar Club, is still in excellent condition. Even before construction started on the new dam, the Dunbar cottage lots held the nucleus of the future Stillwater community.

## The Beaver River Inn Properties

The Dunbars were not the only Stillwater property owners preparing well in advance for the creation of the reservoir. Sometime before 1916, farsighted Harlow Young, owner of the Beaver River Inn, purchased a large Stillwater parcel on higher ground.[6] We do not know whether he somehow had advance knowledge of the future dam or whether he purchased the property for possible expansion of the hotel. We do know that when Young learned of the future dam, he made plans to relocate the Beaver River Inn onto higher ground. As discussed in the last chapter, a significantly remodeled version of that hotel still exists, as does the camp Young built for himself. That camp is now owned by one of his descendants.

In 1919 Young sold a piece of this property to John and Florence Kloster and three other couples.[7] That property is still owned by descendants of one of the families.[8]

## Flooded Lots

Because the state did not purchase the buildings on the property that would be flooded by the new dam, a number of owners appear to have either abandoned their cottages or sold them for salvage.[9] Prior to 1919, there were a handful of other buildings at Stillwater, all situated along the road to the dam.[10] Nearest the dam were the cottages of J. P. Aiids and F. D. Bancroft. A little further back the dam road were the camps of William Fay Smith,[11] Jim Dunbar's nephew, and Jacob Zimmerman. Jimmy Wilder owned a lot right next to the Beaver River Inn, presumably for a boathouse needed for his frequent trips to work as a guide at the Rap-Shaw Club.

Only William Fay Smith and Jacob Zimmerman relocated their camps to higher ground. The camps of J. P. Aiids and F. D. Bancroft and the J. Wilder boathouse were abandoned. The Jim and Lucy Dunbar farm was presumably salvaged.[12] Small parts of the lots of the Kloster group and the lot owned by Foster and Harrington were flooded without damaging the cottages on them.

*New Camps*

Four new camps were built in Stillwater before the end of 1925. Clarence Hicks, Carl Rowley, and former Beaver River guide Carl McCormick all built camps near the hotel, while Fisher Forestry built its own camp on a peninsula on the south side of the hamlet. The Black River Regulating District built a house and office along the shore between the Dunbar cottage lots and the hotel. By the time the reservoir filled in 1925, the hamlet of Stillwater consisted of twelve cottages, the regulating district building, and the reconstructed Beaver River Inn.[13]

**Fisher Forestry and Realty Company**

In June 1925, a feature article titled "Stillwater Likely to Be Big Summer Resort" appeared in a few Central New York newspapers.[14] The article claimed that vacationers from "every section of the Empire state" were rushing to build cottages at Stillwater. The reservoir was praised as "one of the loveliest in the Adirondacks" and the article predicted it was bound to be a magnet for motorboats. Trout fishing was said to be very good since the reservoir and its tributaries had recently been stocked. The article claimed that the state would soon erect a number of public camps on state land.

Reading between the lines, it is clear this article was part of a publicity campaign to sell cottage lots by the Fisher Forestry & Realty Company.[15] By that time Fisher Forestry owned about forty thousand acres along the Beaver River, stretching from the west end of Stillwater to beyond Beaver Lake.

Fisher Forestry had already had considerable success selling cottage lots at Beaver Lake. They even published an illustrated booklet promoting their Beaver Lake development.[16] Clarence Fisher was a frequent summer visitor at Beaver Lake and one of the first to build a camp there in 1904.[17] Many of the other early Beaver Lake cottages were an outgrowth of the vacation cottages at the Fenton House.[18] Today there are forty-three private summer cottages surrounding Beaver Lake.[19] An interesting sidelight is the fact that during the 1930s

Jimmy Wilder, the first steward of the Rap-Shaw Club, was hired to build four Beaver Lake camps and is fondly remembered there.[20]

Fisher Forestry also owned large forested tracts around the west end of the new Stillwater Reservoir, including a large tract on the east side of Twitchell Creek and another large tract on the north side of the Beaver River, containing several beautiful natural lakes. When the 1925 dam was still in the planning stage, Fisher Forestry filed for a restraining order, claiming the new reservoir would cut off road access to these plots and would make sale of lots on these properties impossible. Fisher Forestry discontinued its legal action after the state entered into a settlement that guaranteed access to both areas would be preserved.[21]

As noted above, even before the 1925 dam was finished, Fisher Forestry had sold a few cottage lots at Stillwater. As soon as the dam was

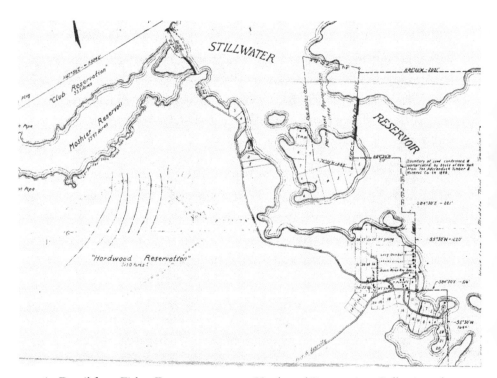

69. Detail from Fisher Forestry map 9093, Hardwood Reservation. Collection of the Hudson River / Black River Regulating District.

completed, they had their remaining property adjacent to the dam surveyed and filed a subdivision map showing projected roads and thirty-eight additional cottage lots. These lots sold slowly but steadily until all were taken. Today's hamlet of Stillwater is composed of seasonal cottages on most of these lots and a small number of year-round homes.

The number of buildings in Stillwater, Beaver River, and Beaver Lake / Number Four has not changed much over time. The primary reason for this stability is a decision made by the state-created Adirondack Park Agency (APA) in 1973 when it approved the Adirondack Park Land Use and Development Plan. In its simplest terms, the plan was designed to channel growth in the park around communities where roads, utilities, and services already existed. That plan divided all privately owned land within the Adirondack Park into six land use classifications, including one called Hamlet.[22] Small lots and dense population are permitted in APA-designated hamlets but not on other private land within the Adirondack Park. There are no APA-designated hamlets in the Beaver River country.[23]

### Stillwater's Public Recreational Facilities

Although the Black River Regulating District made a promise in 1925 to develop public facilities at the Stillwater Reservoir, that promise was not realized for more than fifty years.[24] Shortly after the dam was completed in 1925, the state built a small parking area at the end of the road, and not much else. After the Second World War the state acquired some surplus mats intended for temporary runways in the Pacific and repurposed them as a boat launch. They deteriorated after a few years of use. Until the early 1970s recreational use of the reservoir was light. Those with seasonal camps at Stillwater and Beaver River used the reservoir for fishing and boating and the forest for hunting. There were no designated campsites and few campers.

Terry Perkins was appointed the Stillwater forest ranger in 1967. He continued the traditional ranger's duties, but after the Department of Environmental Conservation (DEC) was organized in 1970, he also set to work dealing with environmental issues. One of his first challenges was to find a way to close the many private garbage dumps and end the practice of dumping all sorts of refuse in the back bays of the reservoir.[25]

The number of people tent camping along the shores of the Stillwater Reservoir slowly increased after 1970. Perkins registered campers and checked on the most popular campsites as time allowed. He performed restoration work on the Red Horse Trail that had gone for decades without maintenance. He also planned and helped construct improvements to the state landing, including the installation of concrete boat ramps, boat docks, an information kiosk, and an outhouse.

In the summer of 1981, an evocative article by Edith Pilcher appeared in the DEC magazine, the *Conservationist*, highly praising canoe camping at Stillwater.[26] Pilcher called Stillwater "the wildest, most beautiful lake in Adirondacks." Terry Perkins remembers that the number of tent campers increased significantly after Pilcher's article was published. To deal with what was becoming overuse of the most popular camping spots, he set up the designated campsite system still in use. Today there are forty-six free primitive campsites around the reservoir available on a first-come-first-served basis. Perkins estimates that the number of visitors camping at the reservoir topped out at about four thousand per year in the 1980s before declining slightly, then climbing back to about four thousand and stabilizing.

Terry Perkins retired as DEC ranger in 1998, but continues to perform some of his former maintenance duties under contract with the DEC. It is impossible to overstate the impact he has had on Stillwater, sometimes in unexpected ways. For example, there is the matter of the road to the dam.

The access road to the parking lot is the only public road in Stillwater. All other roads in the hamlet are on private land. In 1925, the Black River Regulating District (now the Hudson River–Black River Regulating District, or HRBRRD) purchased land from Fisher Forestry and constructed a road to reach the present dam from the landing. The original purpose of this road was to allow regular inspection and service to the dam, but as the hamlet developed residents commonly used this road to reach their camps. Eventually HRBRRD decided that its use of the dam road had become secondary to that of the residents. The supervising engineer in charge of the Stillwater dam announced that he intended to stop maintaining the road and that the residents should take over. A series of angry community meetings followed. One resident repeatedly pointed out that the road belonged to HRBRRD and continued to be necessary for dam operation. One day this resident appeared at the ranger station and asked Terry Perkins to prepare and post a street sign reading "Necessary Dam Road." That is how the road got its name.

### The Stillwater Reservoir Today

Since the end of passenger train service in 1964, the only way to reach the Stillwater Reservoir is by motor vehicle.[27] The western route involves an 18-mile trip from Lowville along the Number Four Road and then another 8.3 miles on the old gravel Carthage-to-Lake Champlain Road to the boat landing. This trip takes about forty minutes from Lowville. From the southeast the Big Moose Road leads 7.8 miles from Eagle Bay to Big Moose Station where the pavement ends. It is 10.3 miles more to the landing on a gravel road. Driving in on this route also takes about forty minutes from Eagle Bay. The routes meet at the parking lot and boat launch at the western end of the reservoir. Anyone headed to Beaver River Station at the eastern end of the reservoir has to take other transportation from the state landing to cross the reservoir.

The Stillwater Hotel is located on the north side of the parking lot. The hotel has a restaurant with a fully stocked bar and is open year-round.

The Stillwater Shop is located just across the access road from the hotel. The shop is a convenience store coupled with an outdoors supply store. The store offers basic groceries, snacks, drinks, and ice, as well as fishing and camping supplies, New York State fishing licenses, books, and area maps. It has boats for rent, ranging from canoes and kayaks to a variety of motorboats. Self-service gas pumps out front offer regular and non-ethanol fuel.

Paul Jacobs established the Stillwater Shop in in 1967. He created the store by converting a house that already stood on the site. Jacobs's daughter, Jean Jenkins, later inherited the property. She and her husband Ray ran the store until 1996, when Frank and Jackie Rudolph purchased it. The Rudolphs refurbished and expanded the property to include a gas station, boat rental, and boat storage facility. Frank Rudolph died in 2017. Daryl and Gail Marsh now own and operate the Stillwater Shop.

At the eastern end of the reservoir, the hamlet of Beaver River still fulfills its historic role as a unique oasis in the wilderness. The hamlet has grown over the years to include about one hundred seasonal camps.[28] It has the distinction of being the only settlement in New York with no direct road connection. It is possible to visit by boat, car ferry, floatplane, or snowmobile. It is also possible to hike from Twitchell Lake, or cross-country ski from Big Moose Station or Stillwater.

The Norridgewock Lodge operated by the Thompson family remains the community center of Beaver River. It offers lodging in five lakeside cabins, four motel rooms, and group accommodations in the historic Norridgewock II hotel. The Norridgewock has a restaurant, serving three meals a day, and a fully stocked tavern.

The Thompsons provide transportation services to those without their own boat. Their car ferry can accommodate up to six cars or trucks at a time. It operates on a reservation-only basis between May and December. They also offer water taxi service from Stillwater to the dock at Grassy Point, the start of the Red Horse Trail, or any of the campsites on the reservoir. They also offer a cruise from Stillwater landing to Beaver River on a custom-made "riverboat." Scott Thompson pilots the boat and provides narration on the history of the reservoir along with personal anecdotes from his life as a Beaver River resident.

Today members of the Thompson family are the only full-time residents of Beaver River. There are a handful of year-round residents at Number Four and a few more at Stillwater. Otherwise, the population of the Beaver River country is made up of seasonal guests. They come with small boats of all kinds in the summer and with snowmobiles in winter.

Although the Stillwater Reservoir was once envisioned as a major tourist mecca, that vision never became a reality. The reservoir is wild and beautiful, but its hidden topography dotted with the many rocky shoals left behind by the glaciers has limited the use of motorboats. The need to travel a long dirt road away from the popular tourist routes has discouraged all but the most determined visitor.

Those who do visit find one of the most beautiful large bodies of water in the Adirondacks, nearly completely surrounded by wild state land. The fishing is good, especially for smallmouth bass. Visitors often form a deep affection for the Beaver River wilderness. Their personal attachment to the welfare of the forest and waters has translated into generations of stewardship, including everything from fish stocking to firefighting to volunteer search and rescue to political advocacy.

One Stillwater seasonal resident recently summed it up like this, "The Beaver River country is still wilderness because anybody can visit and enjoy it but not many can stay."

*Appendixes*

*Notes*

*Bibliography*

*Index*

# Timeline of the Beaver River Country

~4000 BCE—Native Americans begin to inhabit the Adirondack region.

1771—Totten and Crossfield Purchase

1775–83—The American Revolution

1786—New York State Land Commission created to sell "excess property."

January 10, 1792—Alexander Macomb and silent partners William Constable and Daniel McCormick purchase a large part of the Adirondacks.

November 25, 1794—James Greenleaf purchases 210,000 acres of the southern portion of the Macomb Purchase; he mortgages the land to Philip Livingston and gives a second mortgage to John Brown, a merchant from Providence, Rhode Island.

1798—First settlers of European ancestry settle in Lowville, New York.

December 29, 1798—John Brown successfully forecloses on the Greenleaf mortgage; his Adirondack property becomes known as John Brown's Tract.

1812–15—The Albany Road is constructed from the vicinity of Fish House in the south to Russell in the St. Lawrence River Valley.

1822—John Brown Francis finances a road from the Black River to the Beaver River in Township Number Four; settlement of the pioneer village begins.

1825—Erie Canal opens.

1826—Orrin Fenton family moves to Number Four; they begin to provide room and board to passing travelers at their homestead.

1837—Ebenezer Emmons first uses the term "Adirondacks" to refer to the north woods in his report to the New York state legislature.

1844–50—Carthage-to-Lake Champlain Road is cleared from west to east across the Central Adirondacks.

1845—Hermit David Smith departs; Smith's Lake is named for him.

1850—Lyman R. Lyon purchases the unsold land in John Brown's Tract; lumbering begins along the Beaver River.

1850–55—The three Constable family camping trips to Raquette Lake.

1850—Black River Canal begins to operate.

June–July 1851—Jervis McEntee and Joseph Tubby cross the Beaver River country on a sketching trip.

1853—Beaver River is declared a "public highway" for floating logs.

January 1858—James "Jimmy" O'Kane dies; he had lived at Stillwater full-time since 1844.

1859—Chauncey Smith builds a log cabin on the South Branch to accommodate tourists.

1864—*New York Times* publishes its first editorial calling for an Adirondack Park.

1864—A log-driving dam is constructed at the outlet of Smith's Lake.

April 1869—William Henry Harrison Murray publishes the first edition of *Adventures in the Wilderness; or, Camp-life in the Adirondacks.*

1870—Charles Fenton purchases and expands the Fenton House at Number Four.

~1870—William Wardwell purchases fifty acres at Stillwater and builds a pioneer homestead that provides room and board to passing sportsmen.

1871—New York State passes a law that allows the posting of private lands as game preserves and lease of land to private sportsmen's clubs.

1872—Verplanck Colvin begins his Adirondack survey; he strongly advocates for creation of an Adirondack Park.

1873—New York State Commission on Parks recommends a state park in the Adirondacks.

June 1871—H. Perry Smith and friends, including guidebook author Edwin R. Wallace, cross the Beaver River country on an extended camping trip.

1873–79—W. W. Hill makes repeated trips to the Beaver River country for fly-fishing and butterfly collecting.

1878—Joseph Dunbar buys Wardwell's at Stillwater and builds a hotel and guest cabins.

1878—Frank Tweedy draws the first accurate map of the upper Beaver River.

~1878—Andrew Muncy leases fifty acres at Little Rapids and builds a sportsmen's hotel.

1880—New York State hires the first game protectors.

~1880—James Lamont purchases the Edwards's hotel at Smith's Lake.

1885—Legislature establishes the New York State Forest Preserve; a three-person Forest Commission is created to oversee the Forest Preserve.

July 1885—Work begins on the first impoundment dam at Stillwater; dam is completed in 1887.

September 26, 1888—Mary L. Fisher brings suit against New York State for damages to her forest caused by the first Stillwater dam.

1891—Dr. William Seward Webb purchases large parcels of Adirondack land, including all the land around the headwaters of the Beaver River.

1892—Legislature creates the Adirondack Park.

1892—New York State passes law to allow private landowners to arrest trespassers.

October 1892—Passenger service begins on Mohawk & Malone Railroad.

1893—Beaver River Club purchases Dunbar Hotel; Monroe "Pop" Bullock is hired as first club manager.

1893—Webb creates a square parcel of land exactly six-tenths of a mile on each side to create the Beaver River Block.

1893—Firman Ouderkirk opens a lumber mill east of the Beaver River station.

~1893—Chet and William Elliott build the Elliott Camp with the help of Joseph Dunbar near the South Branch of the Beaver River.

1893—W. Seward Webb builds Nehasane Forest Lodge on Smith's Lake, which he renames Lake Lila.

1893–94—Wood and earth dam at Stillwater is replaced and raised five feet to a total height of 14.5 feet.

1894—Webb sues New York State, alleging he cannot float logs down the Beaver River because of the new dam.

1894—Beaver River Club builds a new bridge over Twitchell Creek.

1895—New York State Constitution amended to provide Adirondack Forest Preserve stays "forever wild."

1895—New York State establishes the Fisheries, Game and Forest Commission to take over regulation of forest resources and enforce environmental laws.

January 16, 1896—New York State purchases 74,584.62 acres of Webb lands to add to the Forest Preserve to settle Webb's 1894 lawsuit.

1896—As a condition of the Webb purchase, the Red Horse Trail is improved and extended to the Oswegatchie River at High Falls.

May 1896—The Rap-Shaw Club informally organized.

1899—Firman Ouderkirk purchases the entire Beaver River Block and builds the original Norridgewock Hotel.

1900—New York State changes the name of the Fisheries, Game and Forest Commission to the Forest, Fish and Game Commission.

1901—Monroe "Pop" Bullock builds the Grassy Point Inn with the help of his son Bert.

March 4, 1901—Rap-Shaw Fishing Club incorporated.

1901–May 1902—Rap-Shaw Club is evicted from Webb property at Beaver Dam Pond; buildings are relocated to state land at Witchhopple Lake.

1902—New Beaver River Clubhouse is completed to replace the Dunbar Hotel.

June 1902—Henry C. Churchill replaces Pop Bullock as manager of the Beaver River Club.

1902—Original Norridgewock Hotel and the entire Beaver River plot sold to B. B. "Bert" Bullock.

1902–3—New concrete dam at Stillwater is completed; water level not raised.

May 1906—H. C. Churchill opens the Old Homestead Hotel at Stillwater; Harlow Young hired as the manager of the Beaver River Club.

April 22, 1908—Beaver River Clubhouse burns down; replaced with grander building by spring of 1910.

1908—Forest fire caused by sparks from a train burns everything from Long Lake West (Sabbatis) to Nehasane along the railroad tracks.

1908—Stillwater residents build a wooden signal tower on Stillwater Mountain for fire protection.

1909—Bert Bullock builds a large concrete block stable across the Grassy Point Road from the Norridgewock Hotel; Burt and Ella Darrow build a boardinghouse on private land just east of the station.

1909–10—Bridge over Twitchell Creek for Carthage-to-Lake Champlain Road is replaced but is destroyed by ice during the winter of 1911.

October 20, 1910—Harlow Young purchases the Old Homestead; he renames it the Beaver River Inn.

1911—New York establishes the Conservation Commission to take over enforcement of hunting and fishing laws.

1911—Bill and Hattie Thompson open Loon Lake Lodge.

1912—Wooden Stillwater Fire Tower is first manned by state forest fire observer.

May 8, 1914—Original Norridgewock Hotel burns to the ground and is not rebuilt.

December 8, 1914—Mortgage foreclosure auction on all Beaver River Club property; Stillwater Mountain Club is formed to continue operations.

1916—New York State evicts squatters from the Adirondack Forest Preserve.

1916—Grassy Point Inn is moved next to the railroad tracks near the station; Pop Bullock and Delia Weaver continue to run it, adding a store and post office.

1916—Hattie Thompson and her sons Clinton and Walter reconstruct their sportsmen's lodge on a lot near the train station and rename it The Evergreen.

April 4, 1916—Rap-Shaw Club complies with the state eviction by relocating their camp to Beaver Dam Pond on land rented from Nehasane Park.

1917—Peter Propp constructs a new hotel by renovating and expanding the stable; Louis Beach leases the property and names it the Norridgewock II.

1919—Wooden Stillwater Fire Tower is replaced with current steel tower.

November 29, 1919—Beaver River Club ceases active operation.

1919—Black River Regulating District is formed.

1920—Clinton and Walter Thompson purchase the Norridgewock II.

1922–24—Work begins to raise Stillwater dam to current height; trees are cleared from four thousand acres to be flooded; camps in the low areas are moved to high ground.

1923—Pop Bullock sells his hotel to George Vincent; the next spring Vincent's Hotel burns to the ground.

August 1924—Roger B. Williams Jr. sells his Beaver River Club properties and buys land nearby that would soon become two islands; he moves buildings to the island and uses salvage to build others for his private camp.

November 1924—Beaver River Inn is demolished; salvage used to build a smaller hotel, also named the Beaver River Inn, on nearby higher ground.

February 11, 1925—Gates close at new Stillwater dam, raising the level nineteen feet.

1925—Black River Canal is closed and declared abandoned.

1926—Conservation Commission is renamed the Conservation Department.

May 1928—Douglas J. Purcell and Kate Yousey Purcell buy the Beaver River Inn; they rename it the Stillwater Hotel.

August 1932—Rap-Shaw Club stocks trout in remote lakes near camp using Merrill Phoenix's floatplane.

Spring 1939—Clubhouse at Rap-Shaw Beaver Dam Pond camp burns down.

July 25, 1939—Rap-Shaw Club Board of Directors votes to purchase the Williams Island camp.

1939—Thompson brothers partnership dissolves; Clint Thompson purchases Walter Thompson's share.

October 14, 1940—Beaver River train station burns down and is not rebuilt.

1945—Darrow's Sportsman's Lodge burns to the ground and is not rebuilt.

1950—Stillwater Hotel bought by Emmett and Marge Hill.

1955—Big Moose Station to Stillwater auto road is completed.

1957—Herbie and Annie Nye retire as Rap-Shaw Club stewards after forty years.

1959—First snowmobiles appear in the Beaver River country.

April 1964—Passenger rail service through Beaver River is discontinued.

1964—Clint Thompson dies; Norridgewock II closes.

1965—Stanley Thompson, son of Clint and Jenny Thompson, and his wife, Pat Morgan, build the Norridgewock III at the current location.

1966—Forest Ranger station is built at Stillwater Landing.

April 22, 1970—New York State establishes Department of Environmental Conservation (DEC); takes over regulation and enforcement of environmental laws.

1971—Legislature creates the Adirondack Park Agency.

1972—Dan and Sue Mahoney buy the Stillwater Hotel.

1972—Freight rail service through Beaver River is discontinued.

1973—Adirondack Park Agency approves the Adirondack Park Land Use and Development Plan that prevents hamlet expansion in the Beaver River country.

March 1, 1974—Norridgewock III burns to the ground; it is rebuilt and reopened the same year.

1979—New York State acquires 7,200 acres of the former Nehasane Preserve and demolishes the structures, including Webb's Great Camp Forest Lodge.

1981—Ranger Terry Perkins develops Stillwater campsite registration system; he improves forty-six of the existing shoreline primitive campsites.

1988—State discontinues fire observation at Stillwater Fire Tower and closes it to the public.

1988—Walt and Marion Stroehmer (now Romano) buy the Stillwater Hotel.

July 15, 1995—A violent windstorm blows down thousands of acres of trees south and west of Cranberry Lake; north end of Red Horse Trail is closed beyond Clear Lake.

2001—Drawdown of the Stillwater Reservoir to refurbish the dam.

July 4, 2016—Stillwater Fire Tower is rehabilitated by Friends of Stillwater Fire Tower and reopened to the public.

# List of Rangers
# and Fire Observers

## Stillwater / Beaver River Forest Rangers

1. David L. Conkey (1909–30)*
2. Albert "Burt" Darrow (1912)
3. Raymond Burke (1931)
4. Moses S. Leonard (1932–35)
5. Austin B. Proper (1936–38)
6. Alex "Mac" Edwards (1938–48)
7. Randolph E. "Randy" Kerr (1947–57)
8. William R. "Bill" Marleau (1948–83)
9. Emmett Hill (1950–66)
10. William Richardson, Jr. (1966)
11. Terry Perkins (1967–98)
12. John Scanlon (1998–2008)
13. Luke Evans (2008–15)
14. Matt Savarie (2016–20)
15. Patrick Lee (2020–present)

* David Conkey served as a state fire warden from 1909 until 1912. He was appointed as a forest ranger in 1913, succeeding Burt Darrow.

The above list is derived from Louis C. Curth, *The Forest Rangers: A History of the New York State Forest Ranger Force* (New York: New York State Department of Environmental Conservation, 1987) and from information provided by retired DEC forest ranger Terry Perkins.

**Stillwater Mountain Forest Fire Observers**

1. Eugene Barrett (1912–23)
2. Harry I. Russell (1924)
3. Charles N. Ward (1924–25)
4. A. D. Petrie (1926–27)
5. Clarence Rennie (1928–39)
6. Theodore Jarvis (1940)
7. George Clair (1941–64)
8. Ken Hite (1964–74)
9. Larry Combs (1975)
10. Gary Kincade (1976)
11. Jim Tracy (1977)
12. Mike Strife (1978)
13. David Gates (1979)
14. Larry Strife (1980–81)
15. Les Mahar (1982–88)

List of fire observers provided by James Fox, president, Friends of Stillwater Fire Tower, Dec. 31, 2018. More information and photographs can be found in James Fox, *Stillwater Fire Tower: A Centennial History . . . and Earlier* (New York: Friends of Stillwater Fire Tower, 2019).

# Notes

## 1. The Wild Beaver River Country

1. The region was also part of the original homeland of Algonquian-speaking people until they were displaced by the expansion of the territories of the Mohawks and Oneidas. Stephen B. Sulavik, *Adirondack: Of Indians and Mountains, 1535–1838* (Bovina Center, NY: Purple Mountain Press, 2005), 32.

2. The most commonly accepted definition of wilderness is from the Wilderness Act of 1964, 16 USCS § 1131: "A wilderness, in contrast with those areas where man and his own works dominate the landscape, is hereby recognized as an area where the earth and its community of life are untrammeled by man, where man himself is a visitor who does not remain." This definition has been adopted verbatim in the Adirondack Park State Land Master Plan.

3. The Adirondack Park State Land Master Plan definitions can be found at https://www.apa.ny.gov/state_land/Definitions.htm. A map showing the current distribution and classification of state land in the Adirondacks can be found at http://adirondack.maps.arcgis.com/apps/PublicGallery/map.html?appid=8d68e17d901b42 67a4e411da4eec768e&group=e9b81b8acof24b5080144471c2cbcf9a&webmap=5dec6 8a5ae7f495b893f63296f7964a1.

4. The exact source of the Beaver River is a matter of some dispute. A number of small streams flow into Lake Lila. Shingle Shanty Stream is arguably the largest of these and the only one that can be paddled for any distance in a canoe or guideboat. The tributaries of Shingle Shanty Stream flow from Deer, West, North, and Panther Ponds. The longest branch flows from Pilgrim Mountain to East Pond to Salmon Lake, then to Little Salmon, Lilypad, and Mud Ponds before reaching the main branch of the Shingle Shanty. Because it is not possible to ascend this branch farther than Salmon Lake, Verplanck Colvin called Salmon Lake the source of the Beaver River. See Orlando B. Potter III and Donald Brandreth Potter, *Brandreth: A Band of Cousins Preserves the Oldest Adirondack Family Enclave* (Utica, NY: North Country Books, 2011), 16–18, with detailed map on p. 18.

5. These glacial features, now stripped of soil and vegetation, still lie in wait just under the surface of today's Stillwater Reservoir, creating serious hazards for the unwary boater. For details, see Nathan Vary, "Navigating Stillwater Reservoir," https://sites.google.com/site/stillwaterreservoirnavigation/.

6. This hand-drawn map is in the Colvin papers in the State Archives in Albany and online at https://digitalcollections.archives.nysed.gov/index.php/Detail /objects/10740. The map was actually surveyed and drawn by an assistant, Frank Tweedy, CE.

7. The information on the geology of the Adirondacks is drawn from Bradford Van Diver, *Roadside Geology of New York* (Missoula, MT: Mountain Press Publishing Co., 1985), 1–39, 299–302, 329–32, and 357–62. See also the Adirondack Park Agency website, http://apa.ny.gov/about_park/geology.htm.

8. A finely detailed description of glaciation specific to the formation of the Beaver River country can be found in Potter and Potter, *Brandreth*, 22–30.

9. One of the best short narratives of the effect of glaciation on the Adirondacks can be found in a short film called *A Matter of Degrees* regularly shown at the Natural History Museum of the Adirondacks (The Wild Center) in Tupper Lake, New York.

10. Prior to their dispersal by the Haudenosaunee, Algonquian-speaking people inhabited the St. Lawrence River Valley and adjacent territory. Early French explorers had extensive contact with Algonquians. Sulavik, *Adirondack*, 32–50.

11. Alfred L. Donaldson, *A History of the Adirondacks*, vol. 1 (New York: Century Co., 1921), 1:28. It should be noted that Donaldson's book has been widely criticized for its lack of reliable sources. Its use in this book is limited to material not generally available from other sources.

12. Joseph F. Grady, *The Adirondacks, Fulton Chain–Big Moose Region: The Story of a Wilderness*, 3rd ed. (Utica, NY: North Country Books, 1972), 11.

13. Nathaniel Bartlett Sylvester, *Historical Sketches of Northern New York and the Adirondack Wilderness* (1877; reprint, Peru, NY: Bloated Toe Publishing, 2014), 5–11.

14. Personal discussion with David Kanietakeron Fadden, Aug. 29, 2017, at the Six Nations Iroquois Cultural Center, Onchiota, New York.

15. Lynn Woods, "History in Fragments," *Adirondack Life* (Dec. 1994).

16. Jay Curt Stager, "Hidden Heritage," *Adirondack Life* (Mar./Apr. 2017): 54–66.

17. See Hidden Heritage video, https://www.youtube.com/playlist?list=PLlq7K rGU4-XNpFaFkbVyaCyRNYcuRVqAo.

18. See Philip Harnden, "Whose Land? An Introduction to Iroquois Land Claims in New York State" [pamphlet], American Friends Service Committee, Feb. 2000. See also Cindy Amrhein, *A History of Native American Land Rights in Upstate New York* (Charleston, SC: History Press, 2016).

19. Shortly after the American Revolution, essentially all Mohawk people left the Mohawk River Valley and settled with their relatives on lands along the Canadian border. At the time of the 1850 Census, only 126 Oneida people remained on their home territory, with 700 living in Green Bay, Wisconsin, and 400 near Thames, Ontario. About 250 Onondagas remained on their home territory south of Syracuse, and about 150 more lived elsewhere with their Seneca or Mohawk relatives. There were no Cayuga people in New York except for 125 living with the Seneca. Some 300 Tuscarora people lived on a reservation near Lewiston, New York. The Seneca nation in far western New York retained the greatest population with about 4,000 people living on three reservations. Lewis H. Morgan, *The League of the Iroquois* (1851; reprint, New York: Citadel Press, 1962), 25–33.

20. Melissa Otis, *Rural Indigenousness: A History of Iroquoian and Algonquian Peoples of the Adirondacks* (Syracuse, NY: Syracuse Univ. Press, 2018).

21. Otis, *Rural Indigenousness*, 263.

22. Emmons was relying on Cadwallader Colden's popular *History of the Five Indian Nations* (1727). See Sulavik, *Adirondack*, 92–97.

23. See especially J. Dyneley Prince, "Some Forgotten Indian Place-Names in the Adirondacks," *Journal of American Folk-Lore* (Apr. 1900): 123–28. Prince based his translations on the 1886 dictionary *Lexique de la Langue Alonguine* and on an interview with Mitchell Sabattis, an Algonquian-speaking guide of the late 1800s. Prince states, "The term Rătīrōntăks, 'tree' or 'wood eaters,' as applied to this sect, simply indicates that the Algonquins were essentially forest Indians, in contradiction to the Iroquois, who called themselves Rătinōnsīōnnī, 'those who build cabins.'" Full text can be found at https://www.jstor.org/stable/533802?seq=6#page_scan_tab_contents.

24. Karonhí:io Delaronde and Jordan Engel, "Haudenosaunee Country in Mohawk," *Decolonial Atlas*, https://decolonialatlas.wordpress.com/2015/02/04/haudenosaunee-country-in-mohawk-2/. There is no agreement on the translation of this word. The earliest reference based on the first Mohawk-French dictionary translates it as "that is so." Prince, "Some Forgotten Indian Place-Names," 128. Morgan, *League of the Iroquois*, 472, translated it as "crossing on a stick of timber." Murray Heller, *Call Me Adirondack: Names and Their Stories* (Saranac Lake, NY: Chauncy Press, 1989), 106, claims this word can be translated as "crossing on a log." Local oral tradition in the Beaver River region commonly holds it means "beaver crossing on a log."

## 2. Claiming the Land

1. Amrhein, *History of Native American Land Rights*, 15–17.

2. The Native American concept of territorial occupation as opposed to transferrable land title is discussed in some detail by Robert Gilman, "The Idea of Owning Land," Context Institute, http://www.context.org/iclib/ic08/gilman1/.

3. Details of the Totten and Crossfield Purchase are drawn from Donaldson, *History of Adirondacks*, 1:51–61.

4. The northern line of this tract ran from Keene Valley west to present-day Cranberry Lake, then south on a diagonal taking in Raquette Lake, Blue Mountain Lake, and Indian Lake, among others encompassing most of present-day Hamilton County as well as portions of Warren and Herkimer Counties. See Donaldson map, figure 6.

5. Paul G. Bourcier, *History in the Mapping: Four Centuries of Adirondack Cartography*, catalog of the exhibit, June 15, 1984–October 15, 1984 (Blue Mountain Lake, NY: Adirondack Museum, 1986), 10.

6. A rock bearing carved inscriptions from the Colvin survey party sits just off the Grassy Point Road about a mile from Beaver River Station.

7. For a discussion of the treaties that preceded the Macomb Purchase see Amrhein, *History of Native American Land Rights*, 27–41.

8. Donaldson, *History of Adirondacks*, 1:62.

9. A full description of the controversy surrounding Macomb's Purchase can be found in the New York State *Annual Report of the Forest Commission for the Year 1893*, 2 vols. (Albany: James B. Lyon, State Printer, 1894).

10. The land purchased by Ward was situated in the westernmost portions of Great Tracts V and VI. Shown on Donaldson map, figure 6.

11. Ward's sale to Greenleaf was an extremely convoluted transaction; see Charles E. Herr, *The Fulton Chain: Early Settlement, Roads, Steamboats, Railroads and Hotels* (Inlet, NY: HerrStory Publications, 2017), 3–7.

12. Charles E. Snyder, "John Brown's Tract. An Address by Charles E. Snyder, of Herkimer, Delivered before the Herkimer County Historical Society, December 8, 1896." In *Papers Read before the Herkimer County Historical Society during the Years 1886, 1897 and 1898*, compiled by Arthur T. Smith (Herkimer and Ilion, NY: Citizen Publishing Co., 1899).

13. The story of John Brown's life and Adirondack purchase are from Henry A.L. Brown and Richard J. Walton's exquisitely detailed account, *John Brown's Tract: Lost Adirondack Empire* (Canaan, NH: Published for the Rhode Island Historical Society by Phoenix Pub, 1988).

14. Brown's multiple efforts to settle the tract are detailed in Grady, *Story of a Wilderness*, 13–55.

## 3. Earliest Settlers

1. John Brown Francis (1791–1864) spent much of his adult life deeply involved in politics in Rhode Island, where he served multiple terms in the state legislature. He briefly served in the US Senate and was the thirteenth governor of

Rhode Island from 1833 to 1838. Francis Lake near the hamlet of Number Four is named for him.

2. W. Hudson Stephens, *Historical Notes of the Settlement on No. 4, Brown's Tract, in Watson, Lewis County, N.Y. with Notices of the Early Settlers* (Utica, NY: Roberts, 1864). This work is included as an appendix in Donaldson, *History of Adirondacks*, vol. 2.

3. Clarence L. Fisher, "Adirondack Mountains, Number Four Settlement," *Black River Democrat*, Sept. 21, 1922.

4. See also Christa Caldwell, *This Little Bit of Paradise: Beaver Lake at No. 4* (New York: Lewis County Historical Society, 2015), 13–14. Caldwell suggested Orrin Fenton's possible reason for originally moving to Number Four in correspondence with the author.

5. See W. W. Hill, "The Beaver River Country, N.Y.," *Forest and Stream* 3, no. 1 (August 1874).

6. Some early adventurers did travel at least some distance upstream from Beaver Lake. For example, the first recorded fishing trip above Beaver Lake occurred as early as 1815 or 1816. This party named Sunday Creek. Stephens, *Historical Notes*.

7. Details of the development of Beaver Lake at Number Four can be found in Caldwell, *This Little Bit of Paradise*.

8. Nelson Beach, *Journal of Proceedings Relative to the Carthage and Lake Champlain Road*, transcription by Noel Sherry, collection of the Lewis County Historical Society.

9. Sylvester, *Historical Sketches*, 129–31. Sylvester trained as a lawyer in Lowville, New York, and frequently traveled to the Beaver River country during the late 1850s to hunt and fish.

10. For example, William Marleau, *Big Moose Station* (Van Nuys, CA: Marleau Family Press, 1986), 8.

11. Snyder, "John Brown's Tract."

12. Smith is also mentioned in the State of New York *Second Annual Report of the Commissioners of Fisheries, Game and Forests of the State of New York* (New York and Albany: Wynkoop Hallenbeck Crawford Co., 1896), 152.

13. McEntee's trip is further described in chapter 6.

14. The quotations are from McEntee's diary found in the Blue Mountain Lake Museum research library. Jervis McEntee, "Diary for 1851," manuscript and typescript, MS 67-019, Adirondack Experience Library, Blue Mountain Lake, NY.

15. Sylvester, *Historical Sketches*, 137–39. The 1891 Forest Commission report credits Sylvester as the source for facts about O'Kane. State of New York, *Annual Report of the Forest Commission of the State of New York for the Year Ending December 31, 1891* (Albany, NY: James B. Lyon, State Printer, 1892), 156.

16. Marleau repeats these same facts in *Big Moose Station*, 8–9.

17. "A Month at the Racket" by Bob Racket (pseudonym of John Constable), *Knickerbocker* (1856), reprinted in Edith Pilcher, *The Constables, First Family of the Adirondacks* (Utica, NY: North Country Books,1992), 72.

18. O'Kane's imaginative obituary appeared in the Lowville *Northern Journal* in January 1858, reprinted in Stephens, *Historical Notes*.

### 4. The Red Horse Trail

1. Joseph Poncet's first-person account is reprinted in Dean R. Snow, Charles T. Gehring, and William A. Starna, eds., *In Mohawk Country: Early Narratives about a Native People* (Syracuse, NY: Syracuse Univ. Press, 1996), 93–103.

2. For an excellent discussion of the most probable route, see Paul Jamieson, *Adirondack Pilgrimage* (Glens Falls, NY: Adirondack Mountain Club, 1986), 56–63. See also Sulavik, *Adirondack*, 89–92 with map on p. 86.

3. Jamieson, *Adirondack Pilgrimage*, 62–63; see also Mabel Gregory Walker, "Sir John Johnson, Loyalist," *Mississippi Valley Historical Review* 3, no. 3 (Dec. 1916): 330.

4. Edwin R. Wallace, *Descriptive Guide to the Adirondacks: And Handbook of Travel to Saratoga Springs, Schroon Lake, Lakes Luzerne, George, and Champlain, the Ausable Chasm, the Thousand Islands, Massena Springs and Trenton Falls* (New York: Forest and Stream Publishing Co., 1876), 37.

5. Edwin R. Wallace, *Descriptive Guide to the Adirondacks*, first published as the second half of H. Perry Smith, *Modern Babes in the Woods; or, Summerings in the Wilderness. To Which Is Added a Reliable and Descriptive Guide to the Adirondacks by E. R. Wallace* (Hartford, CT: Columbian Book Co., 1872), 272–73.

6. Big Crooked Lake is referred to on current USGS maps simply as Crooked Lake.

7. Roy E. Reehil and William J. O'Hern, *Adirondack Adventures: Bob Gillespie and Harvey Dunham on French Louie's Trail* (Cleveland, NY: Forager Press, 2012), 4, 10, 16, 19–21, 25–28, 37, 43.

8. Reehil and O'Hern, *Adirondack Adventures*, 100–106.

9. Paul F. Jamieson, *Adirondack Canoe Waters: North Flow* (Glens Falls, NY: Adirondack Mountain Club, 1981), 28–29.

10. These improvements must have occurred after August 1919 because Gillespie's diary does not mention them.

11. Marleau, *Big Moose Station*, 14. Descriptions of these camps are set forth in more detail in chapter 10.

12. Jamieson, *Adirondack Canoe Waters*, 28–29, and personal interview with retired ranger Terry Perkins.

13. Adirondack Mountain Club's *Western Trails* provides a detailed description of the trail as it exists today. Norm Landis and Bradly A. Pendergraft, *Western Trails Book and Map Pack* (Glens Falls, NY: Adirondack Mountain Club, 2016), trail 100, 153–54; this guidebook is revised periodically, so the trail number and pages may change in later editions.

## 5. The Road to Stillwater

1. Charles E. Snyder, "John Brown's Tract."

2. Jamieson, *Adirondack Pilgrimage*, 56–63. See also Sulavik, *Adirondack*, 89–92.

3. Donaldson, *History of Adirondacks*, 1:130.

4. The remains of the bridge are described in McEntee, "Diary," 10–11.

5. A number of early roads along the valleys on the edges of the Adirondacks were built shortly before 1812. Three of these roads are shown on Amos Lay's 1812 *Map of the Northern Part of New York*. This same map shows no roads of any kind anywhere in the Beaver River country.

6. Wallace, *Guide* (1894 ed.), gives the entire route and mileage as follows: Carthage to Belfort, 15; to Number Four, 9; to Stillwater, 11; to South Branch, 7 ¼; to Brandreth, 9 ½; to North Bay of Raquette Lake, 6; to Long Lake Village, 17 ¾; to Newcomb, 13; to Tahawas [Tahawus] Lower Iron Works, 7 ½; to the Schroon River ("Roots"), 19; to Crown Point on Lake Champlain, 19. Total length = 134 miles.

7. The journal kept by Nelson J. Beach during this survey is preserved at the Lewis County Historical Society, Lowville, New York.

8. Franklin B. Hough, *History of Lewis County, New York, with Illustrations and Biographical Sketches of Some of Its Prominent Men and Pioneers* (Syracuse, NY: Mason, 1883).

9. We know the date because E. R. Wallace tells of how Charles Fenton and his brother George were rescued by the road crew after they were lost in the woods for two days between the Beaver River and Brandreth Lake. Wallace, *Guide* (1889 ed.), 400–401.

10. This is the cabin later occupied by Jimmy O'Kane; see chapter 3.

11. For example, John Constable hired a man named Charlie Phelps to clear the brush from Number Four all the way to Raquette Lake in the spring of 1867. Pilcher, *Constables*, 101.

12. For an account of the road specific to the section between the Beaver River and Raquette Lake, see Potter and Potter, *Brandreth*, 31–40.

13. See, e.g., Pilcher, *Constables*, 67, and Caldwell, *This Little Bit of Paradise*, 4.

14. While it may be romantic to imagine an early road had some military use, even the few roads that actually saw some military use in the War of 1812 were constructed mostly for commercial purposes. See Bourcier, *History in the Mapping*, 15.

15. Donaldson, *History of Adirondacks*, 2:123–30. See also Potter and Potter, *Brandreth*, 31–32, and Maitland DeSormo, *The Heydays of the Adirondacks* (Saranac Lake, NY: Adirondack Yesteryears, 1974), 86–90.

16. An interesting notation on the 1818 *Map of the State of New York with Parts of Adjacent States* by John H. Eddy shows an "intended" road starting near Lowville, crossing the Beaver River a mile or so west of Beaver Lake, and joining with the Albany Road near the high falls of the Oswegatchie River. There is no evidence this road was ever built, but Wallace's *Guide* (1894 ed.), 125, does note its possible brief existence.

17. An example of this error can be seen on the 1895 map of Hamilton and Herkimer counties by Joseph Rudolf Bein.

18. A good summary of the course of all the earliest roads along with an excellent map can be found in Barbara McMartin, *To the Lake of the Skies: The Benedicts in the Adirondacks* (Chicago: Lakeview Press, 1996), 20–21. See also the discussion in Potter and Potter, *Brandreth*, 32.

19. Potter and Potter, *Brandreth*, 31.

20. Potter and Potter, *Brandreth*, 39, notes guestbook entries by road travelers essentially ended in 1882, suggesting it had fallen into disuse by then.

21. McEntee, "Diary."

22. Pilcher, *Constables*, 57–91.

23. From Potter and Potter, *Brandreth*, 34–35. The original article appeared in three installments in the *Knickerbocker* in 1856. The entire article is reprinted in Pilcher, *Constables*, 71–88.

24. See descriptions in Smith, *Modern Babes in the Woods*, and A. Judd Northrup, *Camps and Tramps in the Adirondacks, and Grayling Fishing in Northern Michigan: A Record of Summer Vacations in the Wilderness*, (Syracuse, NY: Davis, Bardeen & Co., 1880).

25. "Still Hunting on Vanderwacker (sic) Mountain," *Forest and Stream*, May 27, 1876, reprinted in DeSormo, *Heydays of the Adirondacks*, 92.

26. *Report of the Forest Commission for 1891*, 156. This report also notes that the road could be used from Number Four to Little Rapids but ended there since the bridges were gone all the way to Long Lake.

27. Wallace, *Guide* (1897 ed.).

28. Beach, *Journal*, entries for June 2–June 7, 1841.

29. In 1855, the Constables found the bridge in such disrepair that it was necessary to unhitch the horses and pull the wagons over by hand. "A Month at the Racket," *Knickerbocker* (Sept. 1856), reprinted in Pilcher, *Constables*, 72.

30. None of the sportsmen whose trips are described in chapter 6 used the road beyond Stillwater.

31. Testimony of Andrew J. Muncy before the Fisheries, Game and Forest Commission, *Second Annual Report of the Commissioners of Fisheries, Game and Forests*, 398.

32. Chapter 224 of the *Laws of the State of New York* for 1893.

33. The annual report of the New York State Treasurer for 1909 shows $5,790 spent for Twitchell Creek bridge repairs and the New York State Comptroller's Audit for 1910 shows an additional $1,044 for similar repairs.

34. There was speculation that as late as 1925 the legislature was still considering building a replacement bridge to keep the road in service as far as Beaver River Station. See William B. Donnelly, *A Short History of Beaver River* (private publication for the Beaver River Property Owners Association, 1979), 24.

35. The section of the road from Twitchell Creek to near Beaver River Station is also still in use. It can only be reached by private ferry from the Stillwater landing.

## 6. Sporting Tourists Arrive

1. Glenn Harris, "The Hidden History of Agriculture in the Adirondack Park, 1825–1875," *New York History* 83, no. 23 (Spring 2002): 165–202.

2. Izaak Walton's *The Compleat Angler* was first published in 1653.

3. One indication of the growing popularity of sport fishing is the fact that Charles F. Orvis opened a tackle shop in Manchester, Vermont, specializing in fly-fishing equipment in 1856.

4. Joel T. Headley, *The Adirondack; or, Life in the Woods* (1849; reprint, Bovina Center, NY: Harbor Hill Books, 1982), 442.

5. Headley, *The Adirondack*, 444.

6. A few sporting tourists traveled to the Beaver Lake vicinity as early as 1818. See Stephens, *Historical Notes*, 8–12. The Constable brothers made the first recorded traverse of the entire upper Beaver River from Smith's Lake to Number Four in 1836.

7. The Constable brothers made extensive explorations of the Fulton Chain, Big Moose, the Beaver River, and many of the surrounding waterways in 1833, 1835, 1836, 1839, 1840, and 1843. See Pilcher, *Constables*, 35–39. Their 1843 trip was described in detail in the popular magazine *Spirit of the Times* as "a sporting expedition to Brown's Tract" by Bob Racket (a pseudonym), reprinted in full in Pilcher, *Constables*, 40–49.

8. Pilcher, *Constables*, 37.

9. Bob Racket, "A Month at the Racket," *Knickerbocker* (1856), reprinted in Pilcher, *Constables*, 71–88. The quoted passage appears on p. 88. Pilcher believed Bob Racket was the pseudonym of John Constable.

10. The Clinton Liberal Institute was a classical school in Clinton, New York, operated under the sponsorship of the Universalist Church. McEntee's journal of his school days from August 1844 until October 1845 is in the manuscript collection of Syracuse University.

11. McEntee's journal of this trip is in the collection of the Adirondack Experience museum at Blue Mountain Lake. The details of the weeks in the Beaver River country are from the typescript of the journal; McEntee, "Diary," 1–43.

12. Jervis McEntee, "The Lakes of the Wilderness," *Great Republic Monthly* (Apr. 1, 1859), 335–50.

13. McEntee's detailed observations of O'Kane himself are reported in chapter 3.

14. This was probably the rock shanty near Loon Lake mentioned in many other accounts.

15. Chauncey Smith, a guide from Number Four, had a hunter's shanty at this spot. In 1858–59 he built a log cabin at the same spot that was frequently used by sporting tourists.

16. The two guides on this trip were the same men who guided the Constable parties.

17. Their trip is described in humorous detail in Smith, *Modern Babes in the Woods*, 130–99. Smith does not specify the year of this trip. He does mention Murray's book, however. William H. H. Murray, *Adventures in the Wilderness, or, Camplife in the Adirondacks* (Boston: Fields, Osgood & Co., 1869). Murray's book was first published in 1869. The first trip in Smith's book occurred the year before the Beaver River trip. Smith's book was published in 1872. By process of elimination, the Beaver River trip must have occurred in 1871.

18. Smith describes the cabin in *Modern Babes in the Woods*, 162–63.

19. Smith, *Modern Babes in the Woods*, 179.

20. Smith, *Modern Babes in the Woods*, 197. The travails of H. P. Smith and McEntee are relevant to a recent trespass case brought by Brandreth Park against Phil Brown, the former editor of the magazine *Adirondack Explorer*. Brown made a publicized paddle up part of Shingle Shanty Brook in an attempt to force the owners to remove obstacles and signs prohibiting passage. After extended proceedings, the trial judge sided with the owners, concluding the stream has little historical or prospective commercial use. Michael Virtanen, "Judge Rules for Landowners in Paddling Case," *Adirondack Explorer* (Dec. 21, 2018).

21. Smith, *Modern Babes in the Woods*, 19.

22. Smith, *Modern Babes in the Woods*, 177–78.

23. Hill, "The Beaver River Country, N.Y."

24. The article contains catch records for 13 days of fishing with a total of 592 trout, or 45 per day. The largest catches were 150 on one day, 88 on another.

25. W. W. Hill, "The Beaver River Country," *Forest and Stream* 2, no. 24 (July 23, 1874). Although this article was published first, the family trip of 1873 preceded the trip with his friends.

26. J. A. Lintner, "Mr. Otto Meske's Collection of Lepidoptera," *Transactions of the Albany Institute*, vol. 8 (Albany, NY: J. Munsell, 1876), 215–20.

27. Further details about Hill's life and butterfly collecting can be found in Edward I. Pitts, "Butterfly Effect," *Adirondack Life* (May/June 2020).

28. A report of the collection was published as an appendix to Verplanck Colvin's *Seventh Annual Report on the Progress of the Topographical Survey of the Adirondack Region of New York to the Year 1879* (Albany, NY: Weed, Parsons and Company, 1880). Joseph A. Lintner wrote the introductory remarks to the report and republished it in the State of New York *30th Annual Report on the New York State Museum of Natural History* (Albany, NY: Weed, Parsons and Company, 1879), 141–54.

29. *Annals Entomological Society of America*, vol. 20 (1927), 142. The specimens that Hill collected in the Beaver River country are still housed at the New York State Museum, as are his collecting notebooks.

### 7. First Sportsmen's Hotels

1. Smith speculated that "thousands" of visitors had stayed at the cabin in the fifteen years of its existence; Smith, *Modern Babes in the Woods*, 162.

2. David Fadden of the Six Nations Iroquois Cultural Center in Onchiota, New York, provided this information. An open camp he built has been on display at the museum for many years.

3. Smith, *Modern Babes in the Wood*, 156–57.

4. See, e.g., Joseph Rudolf Bein, *Map of Hamilton, Herkimer counties* (1895).

5. Muncy's name is spelled Muncey or Muncie in some accounts.

6. Some sources spell this name LaMont. I will use the spelling without the second capital letter.

7. Craig Gilborn, *Adirondack Camps: Home Away from Home* (Syracuse, NY: Syracuse Univ. Press, 2000), 71–72.

8. Very little information exists about Muncy's at Little Rapids. The accounts that mention Muncy's do not indicate anything about who may have managed it other than Andrew Muncy.

9. Jervis McEntee made this observation when he stopped at Fenton's on June 12, 1851. McEntee, "Diary," 1.

10. Orrin Fenton also had seven children with his first wife (maiden name Barber) who died, before he remarried and moved to Number Four. It is not recorded how many of these children also lived at Number Four.

11. Stephens, *Historical Notes*, reprinted in Donaldson, *History of Adirondacks*, 2:271. Losee B. Lewis was the son-in-law of Number Four guide Chauncey Smith.

12. Donaldson, *History of Adirondacks*, 2:271.

13. See Wallace's *Guide*, 1872, 1882, and 1888 editions.

14. Hough, *History of Lewis County*.

15. Caldwell, *This Little Bit of Paradise*, 13–16.

16. David Waite, *Entering the North Woods: Beaver River to Lake Lila* (self-published, 2015), 19.

17. Estate of Lyman R. Lyon to William Wardwell, Book 98, p. 22, Herkimer County Clerk's Office, recorded May 1, 1871. This marks the first land transfer at Stillwater other than the sale of the whole township to Lyman R. Lyon from John Brown Frances in 1850. Although the deed was recorded in 1871, the purchase probably occurred in 1870.

18. Waite, *Entering the North Woods*, 18.

19. Smith, *Modern Babes in the Wood*, 156.

20. Northrup, *Camps and Tramps in the Adirondacks*, 135.

21. Hill, "The Beaver River Country, N.Y."

22. Frank Bolles Jr., "A Trip to Albany Lake on Snowshoes," *Forest and Stream* 4 (1875): 197; based on a story told by Charles Fenton.

23. See, e.g., W. W. Ely, *Map of the New York Wilderness* (1876), and S. R. Stoddard, *Map of the Adirondack Wilderness* (1880).

24. According to a brief notice in *Forest and Stream* 6 (May 26, 1876): 251, Charles Fenton reported that Sarah Wardwell had a mental breakdown and had to be confined to an asylum.

25. *Forest and Stream* 6. Also noted by H. H. (Henry Hunn) Thompson, "On the Wilderness Trail," *Forest and Stream* 7 (Sept. 28, 1876): 114.

26. The *Report of the Forest Commission for 1891* refers to Stillwater as Dunbar's.

27. Dannatberg was a village at the location of the Dannat woodworking firm on the bank of Independence Creek. Lewis, Crawford & Company was the largest employer at Chase's Lake, employing ten men full-time. It had a capacity for working 4,000 cords of hemlock bark a year, making about 3,500 barrels of extract. The company also operated two sawmills for cutting the peeled logs into lumber. Hough, *History of Lewis County*, 547.

28. The deeds were not recorded until 1879: William Wardwell to Joseph Dunbar, 10/27/1879—Bk. 115, p. 42. Dunbar also expanded his territory by buying one hundred acres to the south from the Lyon family: Mary B. Lyon to Joseph Dunbar, 01/17/1880—Bk. 116, p. 157.

29. Raymond G. Hopper, "Primeval Adirondacks," *Forest and Stream* 36, no. 22 (June 18, 1891).

30. William F. Morris, "A Trip to the Adirondacks in the Days before Automobiles," *Baldwinsville Gazette and Farmers' Journal*, July 14, 1887.

31. Guides who worked out of Dunbar's included Mark Smith, James Lewis, Chris Wagner, Charles H. Smith, Carl Alger, Henry Simons, Hiram Burke, Isaac Stone, John Hitchcock, Carl Hough, and Emmett Harris. Joseph Dunbar obituary, *Watertown Daily Times*, Apr. 21, 1910.

32. *Watertown Daily Times*, Apr. 21, 1910.

33. *Herkimer Democrat*, Jan. 2, 1889. The Dunbars' arrest was highly unusual for the time. New York did not hire game protectors until 1880. In 1889 there were only eight game protectors patrolling the entire state. Perhaps a complaint of a jealous rival guide or business competitor attracted the attention of the authorities. There appears to be no record of the outcome of the Dunbar trial.

34. Jim Dunbar later worked as a guide for the Beaver River Club and as the first Stillwater dam-keeper. Additional information on his life is in chapter 14.

35. Joseph Dunbar to William Moshier and William Morrison, Mar. 21, 1893, Bk. 147, p. 186.

36. The facts about Muncy's are from his testimony before the Fisheries, Game and Forest Commission in reference to the Webb purchase. A transcript of this testimony can be found in the Charles E. Snyder legal papers in the Adirondack Research Library of the Adirondack Experience Museum at Blue Mountain Lake, 989–1011.

37. Morris, "A Trip to the Adirondacks."

38. In his testimony before the Fisheries, Game and Forest Commission, Muncy explained that after the 1887 dam flooded parts of the Carthage-to-Lake Champlain Road, he had to use a homemade ferry in one place and a floating bridge in another.

39. Smith, *Modern Babes in the Wood*, 179.

40. Wallace, *Guide* (1878 ed.), and Seneca Ray Stoddard, *The Adirondacks: Illustrated* (Albany, NY: Weed, Parsons & Co., 1880), 226.

41. It is difficult to pinpoint the year the Lamonts bought the hotel. They are not mentioned in Wallace's *Guide* of 1878 but do appear in Wallace's 1888 edition, as well as in Whitaker's account of 1886 and Hopper's of 1890. E. S. Whitaker, "Adirondack Tours," *Forest and Stream* 57 (Dec. 7, 1901): 452; Hopper, "Primeval Adirondacks."

42. Hopper, "Primeval Adirondacks," 432–33.

43. See, for example, Whitaker, "Adirondack Tours," 452, and Morris, "A Trip to the Adirondacks."

44. Gilborn, *Adirondack Camps*, 77–78.

45. It was customary for early sporting tourists to refer to guides by their nicknames. Often older guides were referred to as "uncle." These customs are preserved in this book without intending to diminish the many contributions of local guides to the history of the Beaver River country.

46. Goodsell Museum post about Onekio Lodge on Facebook page for the group History and Legends of the Adirondacks, July 25, 2020.

47. *Lowville Journal and Republican*, Jan. 29, 1891.

48. *Lowville Journal and Republican*, June 25, 1891.

49. In 1898 the Lamonts opened a new sportsmen's hotel, Onekio Lodge, on the North Branch of the Moose River. Goodsell Museum post, Facebook page for the group History and Legends of the Adirondacks, July 25, 2020.

## 8. Creation of the Stillwater Reservoir

1. This chapter has benefited substantially from the assistance of Nathan Vary, creator of the comprehensive website, "Navigating Stillwater Reservoir," https://sites.google.com/site/stillwaterreservoirnavigation/.

2. John Brown Francis to Lyman Rasselas Lyon, Herkimer Co. Book of Deeds, Bk. 58, pp. 155, 157. This transaction included all the unsold land in Townships Four and Five of John Brown's Tract.

3. Chapter 643 of the *Laws of the State of New York* for 1853.

4. Michael Williams, *Americans and their Forests: A Historical Geography* (Cambridge: Cambridge Univ. Press, 1992), 174. Barbara McMartin, *The Great Forest of the Adirondacks* (Utica, NY: North Country Books, 1994), 51–54.

5. Chapter 233 of the *Laws of the State of New York* for 1864. This law also directed the Canal Board to levy and collect tolls on all commercial river traffic on the Beaver River, presumably the logs being floated to market.

6. *Second Annual Report of the Commissioners of Fisheries, Game and Forests*, 380, Testimony of William Gibbons. This report contains Dr. Webb's summary of the extensive testimony presented in support of his offer to sell seventy-five thousand acres to the state.

7. Colvin's 1878 map of the Beaver River can be found in the New York State Archives, Verplanck Colvin maps of the Adirondack wilderness, B1405-96, SARA No. 275, 276.

8. Chapter 181 of the *Laws of the State of New York* for 1851.

9. See Noble E. Whitford, *History of the Canal System of the State of New York together with Brief Histories of the Canals of the United States and Canada* (New York: New York State Legislative Printer, 1906). Chapter 9 covers the Black River Canal and Reservoirs on pp. 506–63. There is also a timeline in an appendix.

10. Chapter 336 of the *Laws of the State of New York* for 1881.

11. Galvin would later play a significant role in the founding of the town of Inlet. See Herr, *Fulton Chain*, 45–51.

12. Herr, *Fulton Chain*, 54.

13. Chapter 469 of the *Laws of the State of New York* for 1892.

14. *Second Annual Report of the Commissioners of Fisheries, Game and Forests*, 391.

15. Although the 1894 dam superficially appears similar to a splash dam, the gates were at the bottom and thus could not be opened for log driving. Testimony

in the Webb case made clear this dam could not be modified for log driving. *Second Annual Report of the Commissioners of Fisheries, Game and Forests*, 389–91.

16. Herr, *Fulton Chain*, 55.

17. The Forest Commission was reorganized in 1895 and renamed the Fisheries, Game and Forest Commission. In 1900 it was renamed the Forest, Fish and Game Commission. In 1911 the commission was reorganized again and became the Conservation Commission.

18. Chapter 551 of the *Laws of the State of New York* for 1895.

19. Herr, *Fulton Chain*, 52–56.

20. *Second Annual Report of the Commissioners of Fisheries, Game and Forests*, 417–18.

21. *Second Annual Report of the Commissioners of Fisheries, Game and Forests*, 419–31.

22. A set of restrictions on logging and other commercial uses was a key part of the sale. These restrictions came to be known as the Webb Covenant. Lakeshores were reserved to hotels, camps, cottages, and lumbering. Other commercial, agricultural, or manufacturing uses were prohibited and even logging was limited immediately at lakesides. Existing roads and waterways were kept open to the public. Jane A. Barlow, ed., *Big Moose Lake in the Adirondacks* (Syracuse, NY: Syracuse Univ. Press, 2004), 118; Herr, *Fulton Chain*, 55.

23. As previously mentioned, the state purchased land from Mary L. Fisher in to settle her lawsuit occasioned by the 1887 dam. The state also later acquired significant parcels from Fisher Forestry. Those acquisitions are discussed in chapter 14.

24. Chapter 283 of the *Laws of the State of New York* for 1885.

25. Frank Graham Jr., *The Adirondack Park, a Political History* (New York: Knopf, 1978), 96–106.

26. Chapter 332 of the *Laws of the State of New York* for 1893. When obtaining land for the railroad right-of-way, Webb benefited from obtaining Forest Preserve land in exchange for land elsewhere.

27. Graham, *Adirondack Park*, 126.

28. Graham, *Adirondack Park*, 130.

29. Goodelle was convinced that the state commissioners continued to manipulate the water level of the Beaver River for personal gain. In 1907 he testified before the state Judiciary Committee that Commissioner James P. Lewis was behind the water level fluctuations that were eroding land at the Beaver River Club. *Syracuse Post-Standard*, Mar. 25, 1907, and Lewis's response in the *Watertown Times*, Mar. 29, 1907.

30. Chapter 428 of the *Laws of the State of New York* for 1900. This law was presented as a supplement to chapter 469 of 1892 that authorized the previous dam.

31. A detailed first-person account of the construction of the 1902–3 dam was published in the *Watertown Daily Times*, May 31, 1902. See also the *Paper Mill*, June 7, 1902, 26.

32. "At Stillwater Dam," *Watertown Daily Times*, May 31, 1902. The Santa Clara Lumber Co. owned this property. They had purchased it from Lyman R. Lyon years earlier. In 1905, Mary Lyon Fisher, daughter of Lyman R. Lyon, purchased back the remaining acreage still owned by the Santa Clara Lumber Co. adjacent to the Beaver River.

33. The 1894 dam was visible between 1924 and 1925 when the water was lowered to build the current dam. It also reappeared in 2001 when the reservoir was drained to make repairs to the dam.

34. Whitford, *History of the Canal System*. The Black River Canal and reservoirs are covered in pp. 506–63 and an appendix provides a complete timeline of the damming of the Black River watershed.

35. Graham, *Adirondack Park*, 198.

36. Roscoe C. Martin, *Water for New York* (Syracuse, NY: Syracuse Univ. Press, 1960), "The Black River War," 146–72.

37. P. F. Schofield, "The Forest and Water Storage Policy of the State of New York," *Board of Trade Journal* 40–41 (Jan. 3, 1914): 5–9.

38. Report of Forest Commission for 1917, 78.

39. The Hudson River Regulating District was formed in 1922 and set to work planning the Sacandaga Reservoir.

40. Graham, *Adirondack Park*, 199. Graham explains the process by which both proposed Moose River reservoirs were defeated on pp. 199–207. For a blow-by-blow account of the battle against the Moose River dams, see Paul Schaefer, *Defending the Wilderness: The Adirondack Writings of Paul Schaefer* (Syracuse, NY: Syracuse Univ. Press, 1989), 63–126.

41. Sheet 8 of this set of Stillwater maps is of particular interest. This map shows the lots and buildings of the Beaver River Club as they existed in 1924 before the water rose. This same map shows the outlines of today's Williams, Chicken, Hotel and State Islands. The new Hotel and State Islands were too small to be marketable, so title to them was taken by the state. Only the land on the new Williams and Griffin (now Chicken) Islands remained in private hands.

42. About two hundred acres of land on both sides of the Beaver River at the easternmost end of the reservoir was flooded between Little Rapids and Nehasane Lake. Because of the objections of the three powerful adjoining landowners, the state did not purchase these flooded lands outright; rather it purchased easements allowing the land to be flooded for reservoir purposes only. See, e.g., Memorandum of Agreement between the Ne-ha-sa-ne Park Association and the State of New York, Herkimer County Clerk's Office, Book 287, p. 32, May 31, 1928. Similar easement agreements were reached with the other two landowners: John N. McDonald, and the Brandreth Lumber and Improvement Co. A map of lands to be flooded is filed in

Herkimer County Clerk's Office, Map Book 132, p. 1, with a copy attached to each easement agreement.

43. The relocation of buildings in the Stillwater area is discussed in detail in chapter 14. For relocations near Beaver River Station, see Pat Thompson, *Beaver River: Oasis in the Wilderness* (Beaver River, NY: Beaver River Press, 2000), 31.

44. *Lowville Journal and Republican*, Sept. 1, 1921.

45. Attorney A. H. Cowie represented Beaver River Club lot owners Roger B. Williams Jr., Nellie Chase, Harry T. Hughes, William S. Foster, William L. Dingman, and Charles McCormick.

46. Lester Griffith and Hattie M. Griffith to Wilson D. Ogsbury of Watertown, Book of Deeds 257, p. 245, Jan. 9, 1922.

47. Board of the Black River Regulating District v. Wilson Ogsbury, 203 A.D. 43 (1922), affd. 235 N.Y. 600 (1923).

48. Wilson D. Ogsbury to the state of New York (land below the high-water line), 07/28/1924—Bk. 270, p. 534, and Wilson D. Ogsbury to Roger B. Williams, Jr. and Louise Miller Williams of Ithaca (land above the high-water line), 08/04/1924—Bk. 272, p.165.

49. Martin, *Water for New York*, 151–52.

### 9. Dr. Webb and His Railroad

1. Webb's biography is mainly drawn from Charles Howard Burnett, *Conquering the Wilderness: The Building of the Adirondack & St. Lawrence Railroad by William Seward Webb, 1891–92* (Norwood, MA: Privately printed by Mrs. W. Seward Webb, 1932), 79–80.

2. The elder Webb was wealthy and politically well connected. He was ambassador to Brazil from 1861 until 1869. It is said William Seward Webb was named after William Henry Seward, who served as New York governor 1839–42 and later as Lincoln's secretary of state. When governor, W. H. Seward pardoned James W. Webb just before he was to start a two-year prison term for participating as a second in a duel.

3. In 1888 the firm name was changed to W. S. Webb & Co.

4. There is substantial literature on Dr. Webb's railroad. In addition to Burnett, see Michael Kudish, *Railroads of the Adirondacks: A History* (Bovina Center, NY: Purple Mountain Press, 1996) and *Mountain Railroads of New York State, Volume Two: Where Did the Tracks Go in the Central Adirondacks?* (Bovina Center, NY: Purple Mountain Press, 2007); John M. Ham and Timothy R. Mayers, *The New York Central in the Adirondacks* (Hunter, NY: Stony Clove & Catskill Mountain Press, 2015); and Henry A. Harter, *Fairy Tale Railroad* (Utica, NY: North Country Books, 1979).

5. It is not clear where Webb obtained the money for this large enterprise. Most commentators assume that the Vanderbilt family provided all or part of the funds.

6. Webb also needed to make a separate purchase of the land immediately surrounding Smith's and Albany Lake from William Morrison. That purchase is discussed in chapter 11.

7. Sally E. Svenson, *Blacks in the Adirondacks: A History* (Syracuse, NY: Syracuse Univ. Press, 2017), 73–82.

8. Burnett, *Conquering the Wilderness*, 42.

9. Duncan H. Cameron, "Adirondack Railways: Historic Engine of Change," *Adirondack Journal of Environmental Studies* 19, no. 1 (2013): article 4.

10. Harvey Kaiser, *Great Camps of the Adirondacks* (Jaffrey, NH: David R. Godine, 1982), 195–97. This property still exists largely intact. A pass is required to access the road beyond the gatehouse.

11. Burnett, *Conquering the Wilderness*, 23.

12. "Dr. William Seward Webb's Great Park," *New York Times*, Jan 31, 1895.

13. The name for Webb's preserve is usually written without hyphens.

14. Robinson also worked for Dr. Webb at Shelburne Farms, his country estate in Vermont, and had designed Robert C. Pruyn's Great Camp Santanoni in 1888.

15. Nehasane Preserve is described in detail in Gladys Montgomery, *An Elegant Wilderness: Great Camps and Grand Lodges of the Adirondacks, 1855–1935* (New York: Acanthus Press, 2011), and Kaiser, *Great Camps*, 183–87.

16. "Game Preserve Thrown Open," *New York Times*, Dec. 26, 1903.

17. Barlow, *Big Moose Lake*, 18.

18. On Pinchot and scientific forestry, see McMartin, *Great Forest*, 122–27.

19. As a result of his work at Nehasane, Pinchot published *The Adirondack Spruce* (1898), a classic text on scientific forest management.

20. See McMartin, *Great Forest*, 208–9, for a review of timber harvesting at Nehasane.

21. *Lowville Journal and Republican*, Dec. 23, 1897.

22. Donnelly, *History of Beaver River*, 24. The tote road led from Wallace's lumber camp on the south branch of the Beaver River to Grassy Point. It continued on the north side of the river, skirting the east end of Burnt Lake. Halfway between Trout Pond and Salmon Lake it veered northwest toward the west branch of the Oswegatchie River.

23. The Beaver River train station burned down on Oct. 14, 1940, and was not rebuilt.

24. The line later added flag stops immediately north of Beaver River at Little Rapids and Brandreth. These two stops were created when Webb sold 1,140 acres at Little Rapids to Dr. Edward Trudeau in 1896 and the Thayer Lake tract to the Brandreth family in 1897.

25. Barlow, *Big Moose Lake*, 118, and Herr, *Fulton Chain*, 55.

26. Before 1899, Ouderkirk rented land from Dr. Webb; see Thompson, *Beaver River*, 33.

## 10. Beaver River Station

1. "Webb in the Adirondacks," *New York Times*, Aug. 23, 1891.

2. Karl Jacoby, *Crimes against Nature: Squatters, Poachers, Thieves and the Hidden History of American Conservation* (Berkley, CA: Univ. of California Press, 2001), 40. Around the same time, the Adirondack League Club had twenty game wardens who carried badges that read "police guide."

3. The *Report of the Forest Commission for 1893* cited Nehasane as an example of how quickly the Adirondacks were being closed to the public. After reprinting copies of Webb's no trespassing signs, the report concluded, "these trespass signs are fast becoming a prominent feature of the Adirondacks. They meet the eye whenever one crosses land that is not owned by the State" (289).

4. Regarding Nehasane, see *Report of the Forest Commission for 1893*, 169. A 1910 Beaver River Club advertising brochure claimed the club was always open to the public on application.

5. Jacoby, *Crimes against Nature*, 41–42. For details regarding revenge fires, see p. 73. The famous murder of Orrando Dexter occurred on Sept. 20, 1903, in Franklin County.

6. William "Bing" Elliott eventually became the proprietor of the Central Hotel in Lowville. He died unexpectedly in 1913. *Black River Democrat*, Nov. 13, 1913.

7. *Lowville Journal and Republican*, July 20, 1893.

8. *Utica Observer*, Apr. 2, 1898. The same assessment is repeated in Thompson, *Beaver River*, 35.

9. L. A. Withington, "Deer Hunt in the Adirondacks," *Ogdensburg Daily Journal*, Dec. 4, 1903.

10. See, for example, *Utica Observer*, Apr. 2, 1898.

11. *Brookfield Courier*, June 5, 1912. The Johnsons renamed the property Beaver River Camps. Their camp continued to operate until 1916 when all squatters were removed from state land.

12. Advertisement in *Utica Daily Press*, July 14, 1913.

13. Jacoby, *Crimes against Nature*, 33–34.

14. Reehill and O'Hern, *Adirondack Adventures*, 64–67.

15. The Conkeys later moved to Beaver River Station. Dave Conkey became a fire patrolman in 1909 and a forest ranger in 1913, a position he held until his retirement in 1930. Marleau, *Big Moose Station*, 209–10.

16. Marleau, *Big Moose Station*, 14, and Thompson, *Beaver River*, 36.

17. That Ouderkirk built the original Norridgewock is based on an uncredited newspaper article reprinted in Thompson, *Beaver River*, 33. The earliest mention of the hotel is in an advertisement in the *Utica Daily Press* in May 1899, noting B. B. Bullock as the manager with rates of $7–$10/week.

18. Donnelly, *History of Beaver River*, and Thompson, *Beaver River*.

19. George J. Varney, "History of Norridgewock, Maine," *A Gazetteer for the State of Maine* (Boston: B. B. Russell, 1886).

20. William L. Wessels, *Adirondack Profiles* (Lake George, NY: Adirondack Resorts Press Inc., 1961), 82.

21. *Lowville Journal and Republican*, May 9, 1907, and June 13, 1907. Louis Beach was the brother of Henry M. Beach, the renowned Adirondack photographer who then had his studio in Lowville. See Robert Bogdan, *Adirondack Vernacular: The Photography of Henry M. Beach* (Syracuse, NY: Syracuse Univ. Press, 2003).

22. *Sandy Creek News*, Aug. 12, 1909.

23. This fancy cash register still sits behind the bar at the current Norridgewock.

24. For more about Pop Bullock and Delia Weaver, see Edward Pitts, "Pop Bullock: Notable Beaver River Guide," *Adirondack Almanack*, Feb. 3, 2018.

25. Bill Gove, *Logging Railroads of the Adirondacks* (Syracuse, NY: Syracuse Univ. Press, 2006), 83–85.

26. *New York Times*, May 13, 1924. The story passed down by Beaver River locals is that Vincent died when he rushed back into the burning building to try to retrieve a guest's luggage.

27. Thompson, *Beaver River*, 45–48, photo, 50.

28. Louis C. Curth, *The Forest Rangers: A History of the New York State Forest Ranger Force* (Albany: New York State Department of Environmental Conservation, 1987), 210. David Conkey is often cited as the first Beaver River forest ranger. Conkey served as a fire warden from 1909 until 1912. He was appointed as a forest ranger in 1913, succeeding Burt Darrow.

29. Donnelly, *History of Beaver River*, 42.

30. Pat Hartman, *A Butcher in Beaver River: Edwin Butcher in the Adirondacks* (privately published, 2017), 20. I am grateful to Ms. Hartman from Niagara-on-the-Lake, Ontario, for sharing her account of the life of her ancestor Edwin Butcher who lived in Beaver River Station throughout the 1920s. Hartman's account is on file at the Goodsell Museum in Old Forge, New York.

31. Donnelly, *History of Beaver River*, 25.

32. The Thompsons were not the original builders of the Loon Lake Lodge. A photo postcard in the collection of Tim Mayers postmarked May 4, 1907, shows the same building was then called Camp Lookout. No further information on this earlier camp has been found.

33. Thompson, *Beaver River*, 28 with photo. Donnelly, *History of Beaver River*, 37.

34. This subtitle is borrowed from Thompson's memoir, *Beaver River*. Pat and her husband, Stanley, are discussed later in this chapter in connection with the Norridgewock II and III.

35. *Lowville Journal and Republican*, Nov. 18, 1915. It was estimated there were seven hundred squatters on Forest Preserve land at the time. By the following spring the Conservation Commission had contacted all but 255 of these squatters. Some 104 cases were headed to court, 265 cases were completely closed, fifty-nine had agreed to move in a reasonable time, forty-two owners of tent platforms deeded their platforms to the state and applied for leases, and sixty-five cases were in negotiation. *Lowville Journal and Republican*, Mar. 15, 1916.

36. The Rap-Shaw Club relocated their camp at Witchhopple Lake to Beaver Dam Pond on Nehasane Park. See discussion in chapter 12.

37. Donnelly, *History of Beaver River*, 22.

38. Donnelly, *History of Beaver River*, 52. Beach's 1918 draft card lists him as a hotel proprietor, as does his 1918 state liquor license.

39. Donnelly, *History of Beaver River*, 52.

40. Thompson, *Beaver River*, 26. The Annex, minus its porches, still stands. The sidewalk that led from the train station to the original Norridgewock still leads to the door of the Annex.

41. Gladys Kempton's mother served as postmistress.

42. Donnelly, *History of Beaver River*, 38.

43. Donnelly, *History of Beaver River*, 38, says Walter and Gladys moved to Vermont, but the US Census has them living in Fort Edward, New York, in 1940.

44. Thompson, *Beaver River*, 80.

45. The Norridgewock II sat vacant until Arthur Stadtmiller purchased it in 1971. In 1975 it was purchased by David Crowley and Craig Smith and renamed the Beaver River Hotel. See Donnelly, *History of Beaver River*, 26. The building changed hands again in 2011. It was partly renovated and renamed the Beaver River Lodge. It operated on a part-time basis until it closed again in 2016.

46. Thompson, *Beaver River*, 131–32; Donnelly, *History of Beaver River*, 38.

47. Donnelly, *History of Beaver River*, 125–29.

48. Donnelly, *History of Beaver River*, 134.

49. Donnelly, *History of Beaver River*, 135.

50. Donnelly, *History of Beaver River*, 141.

51. *Utica Observer Dispatch*, Oct. 8, 1923, 8.

52. See Marleau, *Big Moose Station*, 214–17.

53. Niki Kourofsky, *Adirondack Outlaws: Bad Boys and Lawless Ladies* (Helena, MT: Farcountry Press, 2015), 98–99.

54. For more on Jessie Elliott's life, see Edward Pitts, "'Wild Jess' Elliott: Setting the Record Straight," *Adirondack Almanack*, Apr. 15, 2018.

55. By 1925 there were fifteen camps in Beaver River Station. The seven moved from land to be flooded brought the total to twenty-two. *Watertown Daily Standard*, June 13, 1925.

## 11. The Beaver River Club

1. See especially Kaiser, *Great Camps*, and Gilborn, *Adirondack Camps*.

2. The argument for the importance of Adirondack sportsmen's clubs is convincingly laid out in Barbara McMartin, *The Privately Owned Adirondacks: Sporting and Family Clubs, Private Parks and Preserves, Timberlands and Easements* (Chicago: Lakeview Press, 2004).

3. Three of the largest of these early clubs are still in existence today. The largest of all, the Adirondack League Club, encompassing 104,000 acres, was founded near Old Forge.

4. A good discussion of the shortcomings of hotel guides can be found in Charles Brumley, *Guides of the Adirondacks: A History* (Utica, NY: North Country Books, 1994), 18–23.

5. *Report of the Forest Commission for 1893*, 154

6. *Lowville Journal and Republican*, Jan. 29, 1891.

7. *Lowville Journal and Republican*, June 25, 1891.

8. The names of the original members are listed in newspaper accounts in the *Syracuse Evening Courier*, Feb. 11, 1893, and the *Boonville Herald*, Feb. 16, 1893.

9. This land was owned by Mary Lyon Fisher, who had inherited it from her father, Lyman R. Lyon. Lyon purchased most of Township Five of John Brown's Tract in 1850 from the Brown family.

10. The Snell map is filed in the Herkimer County Clerk's Office, Book 8 of maps, p. 23.

11. See, for example, Ken Sprague, "The Beaver River Club," *Adirondack Express*, Nov. 13, 2012, and Seaver Asbury Miller, "The Sporting Clubs in the Adirondacks," *Outing* 32 (1914): 475–82.

12. *Rome Daily Sentinel*, Oct. 31, 1900.

13. *Rome Daily Sentinel*, Oct. 29, 1902.

14. The 1901 supplemental map was drawn for William. K. Pierce. It shows the names of owners of twenty-six lots. This map is filed in Herkimer County Clerk's Office, Book 9 of maps, p. 7.

15. *Syracuse Sunday Herald*, Sept. 8, 1895. Bubble pipes and soap solution had only recently been commercially introduced and were for a time a popular fad at social gatherings.

16. Moshier later played an important role in the development of the Adirondack village of Inlet; see Herr, *Fulton Chain*, 229–34.

17. Rufus J. and his younger brother S. Brown Richardson were founding members of the Beaver River Club. Rufus was elected vice president of the initial board of directors. Rufus founded R. J. Richardson & Co. This successful cheese factory later became Lowville Cold Storage and even later the Kraft Cheese factory still in operation today.

18. As noted in chapter 8, Goodelle played an important role in drafting the constitutional amendment intended to keep the Adirondack Forest Preserve "forever wild."

19. *Rome Daily Sentinel*, July 9, 1904

20. Churchill also built a camp for his family near the eastern end of the first bridge from the mainland in an area now called State Island. Churchill named his camp "Forest Home" in an ironic nod to Dr. Webb, who called the main building at his Great Camp "Forest Lodge."

21. Renowned architects Asa Merrick and James Randall of Syracuse were selected to design the new clubhouse. *Lowville Journal and Republican*, Sept. 24, 1908.

22. Frederick W. Barker was a well-known Syracuse banker and a close friend of James J. Belden, a club member.

23. This brochure is in the Dennis Buckley collection that also contains a very similar brochure for the Beaver River Inn.

24. *Watertown Daily Times*, Dec. 19, 1910.

25. *Syracuse Herald*, June 14, 1911.

26. Foreclosure was granted by the Onondaga County Supreme Court, Oct. 22, 1914.

27. On Dec. 28, 1914, the *Syracuse Journal* reported that "Robert Dey, Alvin J. Belden and Carlton A. Chase with Martin Besemer of Ithaca and William S. Foster of Utica are directors of the Stillwater Mountain Club, the incorporation papers of which were filed in the county clerk's office this morning." The *Utica Herald-Dispatch* reported the same news the next day.

28. A copy of the advertising brochure is in the collection of the Adirondack Experience Museum. Some photographs taken for advertising purposes identify the club property as Dobson's. A small notice for Dobson's at Beaver River also appeared in the annual list of Sporting and Vacation Places published in *Field and Stream* 21 (Aug. 1916): 565.

29. Wetmore specifically reserved personal use of the sawmill that was located on the property.

30. All of this information is from the 1921 set of maps of lands to be flooded prepared by the Black River Regulating District and filed with the Herkimer County Clerk's Office.

31. Part of the only Beaver River Club cottage that was not demolished or moved is still in use on Chicken Island, now part of the Rap-Shaw Club.

32. Full details of Williams's camp are set forth in Edward Pitts, *The History of the Rap-Shaw Club: 1896 until 1958* (self-published, 2019), chap. 16.

33. The foundation of the clubhouse can still be explored on what is now called Hotel Island.

## 12. The Rap-Shaw Club

1. Much more detail about the Rap-Shaw Club can be found in Pitts, *History of the Rap-Shaw Club*. It expands upon the club history provided here, and tells many personal stories, including biographical sketches of the club's founders and first stewards, the tale of two lost fishermen in 1909, a heroic rescue after a serious hunting accident in 1925, and the antics of beloved member D. E. Hartnett.

2. This account by Rapalje appears in the first book of board minutes just before the minutes of the 1916 annual meeting.

3. Philip G. Terrie, *Wildlife and Wilderness: A History of Adirondack Mammals* (Bovina Center, NY: Purple Mountain Press, 1993), 81–95.

4. Rapalje's written recollections of the first trip in May 1896 says that the group included "two from Fairport and three from Elmira." Leander Shaw was one of the Fairport fishermen. A newspaper article titled "Fish, Fish, Fish, Fish" that appeared in the *Elmira Star Gazette*, June 3, 1896, lists the other participants as Harry P. Beebe from Buffalo, Chester E. Wilcox from Fairport, and John J. Hickey, Robert H. Walker, and John Deister from Elmira.

5. Rapalje's notes say that Elliott's Camp was located at Grassy Point, but all other references, maps, and photographs place it farther upstream on the Beaver River near its confluence with the South Branch.

6. Marleau, *Big Moose Station*, xii.

7. The name was formally adopted at the time the club incorporated in 1901. Rapalje recalled the suggestion to keep using the name Rap-Shaw was made by J. N. Elwood.

8. Two captioned 1897 photographs in the Rap-Shaw photo album show Wattles and Pierce. Pierce was the brother of William K. Pierce, a member of the Beaver River Club.

9. This account is from "Fish, Fish, Fish, Fish," *Elmira Star Gazette*, June 3, 1896.

10. Current maps call this lake simply Crooked Lake.

11. See, e.g., Gilborn, *Adirondack Camps*, 47, 51, 57, and 93.

12. Apparently, the founders intended to name the club the Rap-Shaw Fishing *and Hunting* Club but failed due to some miscommunication.

13. The club had seventeen charter members at the time of incorporation. Membership jumped to fifty within the first year. The names of the charter members are in Rapalje's typed account in volume 1 of the Rap-Shaw Club photo album.

14. This meeting is recorded in Rapalje's typed account in volume 1 of the Rap-Shaw Club photo album.

15. The title "steward" dates back to the eleventh century. It originally referred to the person who supervised a lord's estate in their absence. During the nineteenth century in America the term was commonly applied to a person who assisted train passengers, also referred to as a porter. There is no record of why this title was chosen, but it remains in use at the club today.

16. See discussion of removal of camps on Forest Preserve land in chapter 10. It appears that the only camps relocated were Dave Conkey's camp and the Rap-Shaw Club. Elmer Wilder's popular Camp Happy on Salmon Lake was abandoned and destroyed. *Lowville Journal and Republican*, Oct. 16, 1916.

17. Wilder continued work for the club as a guide for many more years.

18. If more than forty club members used the club, an additional ten dollars per member would be added to the rent, up to use by sixty members. If more than sixty members used the club in any year, an additional five dollars per member would be added to the rent, up to a limit of one hundred members.

19. Some of the original guest registers are in the club archive. The limits were never exceeded in the first five years. Nehasane then discontinued the requirement to inspect the guest register.

20. This section of the lease also required the club to purchase and maintain a designated list of firefighting equipment, including collapsible buckets, various rakes, shovels, mattocks, and axes, as well as a supply of food adequate to feed ten firefighters for two days. This explains the presence of the antique firefighting equipment still displayed in the club dining hall.

21. Charles Knipp was the club member who built a private cabin at Witchhopple Lake. The club bought his cabin in 1916 and moved it to Beaver Dam Pond.

22. Denis E. Hartnett, a club member from 1908 until 1947, was a professional musician, amateur poet, practical joker, and untiring booster of the Rap-Shaw Club. His many contributions to the Rap-Shaw Club are described in Pitts, *History of the Rap-Shaw Club*, 67–77.

23. Walker, Clear, and Little Rock Lakes are all located on state Forest Preserve land and are thus under the jurisdiction of the Conservation Department.

24. The story of the club's first aerial fish stocking was published in a different form in the *Adirondack Almanack*. Edward Pitts, "Historic Firsts: Aerial Fish Stocking of Adirondack Waters," *Adirondack Almanack* (May 31, 2017).

25. Phoenix was an Adirondack bush pilot who flew out of Wood's Hotel in Inlet. Floatplanes appeared on the Fulton Chain in 1926 and became a popular tourist

attraction by 1929. See Elizabeth Folwell, "Our Air Force: A Who's Who of North Country Aviators," *Adirondack Life* (Sept./Oct. 2004).

26. Marleau, *Big Moose Station*, 14.

27. The club used the services of a commercial air service on Fourth Lake owned by Al Brussel and Harold Van Auken, often with Merrill Phoenix as pilot.

28. The boys were Bill Marleau and Bill Partridge. Partridge was the son of the Beaver River stationmaster. Marleau later became the Beaver River / Big Moose forest ranger.

29. Terry Perkins told this story during an interview at the Stillwater Hotel in the winter of 2015. He said Marleau related this to him personally when Perkins was the Stillwater ranger.

30. This name is the only indication at the time that the buildings on Williams Island were once part of the Beaver River Club, later also known as the Stillwater Mountain Club. There is no other evidence that members of the Rap-Shaw Board were aware of this connection at the time the club purchased the island property. Roger B. Williams's connection to the Beaver River Club and his purchase of the island is described at the end of chapter 11.

31. These transactions are all reflected in detail in an abstract of title prepared by H. J. Nichols of the Central New York Abstract Corp. dated June 27, 1940, found in the Rap-Shaw Club archives held by the Goodsell Museum in Old Forge, New York.

32. This information is derived from a copy of the 1939 real estate advertisement in the club archive and from an article in the *Watertown Daily Standard*, June 13, 1925. The identical story appeared in the *Lowville Journal and Republican* on June 25, 1925, and in the *Rome Daily Sentinel* on June 29, 1925. A similar story appeared in the *Utica Daily Press*, July 25, 1925.

33. Minutes of the annual meeting held on December 10, 1949, at the Hotel Buffalo. At that meeting board member Arnold Baehre agreed to assume responsibility for paying off a one-thousand-dollar loan the club had taken out the previous January.

34. Special assessments of ten dollars per member were levied in 1950, 1951, and 1952. In 1953 the club took out a mortgage to cover a shortfall of $1331.29. Special assessments were levied occasionally for the remainder of the 1950s.

35. Description of the first formal fishing contest is from F. Russell Hyde, "Fishing Trophies," *Rap-Shaw Review* 1, no. 2 (June 1950).

36. F. Russell Hyde, "Trophies Awarded! Fishermen, Hide Your Heads," *Rap-Shaw Review* 1, no. 3 (Oct. 1950).

37. These two fine brass trophies now reside above the fireplace in the club's dining hall. They were awarded every year from 1950 until 1955.

38. The Big Boat story appears in volume 1 of the Rap-Shaw Club photo album, p. 49.

39. In 1964 the "Big" was considered unsafe and was towed to a deep part of the Flow, burned, and scuttled.

40. A s'more is a traditional campfire treat popular in the United States and Canada, consisting of a fire-roasted marshmallow and a layer of chocolate sandwiched between two pieces of graham cracker.

## 13. Stillwater Hotels

1. Jim Fox provided the personal details of the Churchill family. His wife Carol Shaver Fox is Churchill's great-granddaughter.

2. See advertisement for Stanton's Camp in the *Utica Daily Press*, June 22, 1901. Stanton's was located on the north shore of the Beaver River a few miles upstream from Stillwater.

3. Churchill must have owned this boat. According to an early Old Homestead advertising brochure in the Shaver / Fox collection, he continued to use it to transport guests after he opened the Old Homestead. He sold the boat to Harlow Young when Young bought the hotel.

4. Guest registers from the Beaver River Club, the Old Homestead, and the Beaver River Inn are in the collection of the Goodsell Museum of the Town of Webb Historical Association in Old Forge. H. C. Churchill's great-granddaughter, Carol Shaver Fox, donated the Beaver River Club register. Eugene Buckley, a relative of Harlow Young, donated the Old Homestead and Beaver River Inn registers.

5. There were five Stickley brothers who made furniture in the United States. They originally all worked together in Central New York at the Stickley Brothers Furniture Co., managed by brothers Gustav, Albert, and Charles. Gustav eventually opened Craftsman Workshops and became one of the leading proponents of the Arts and Crafts Movement in America.

6. Harlow Young's great-great-nephew, Dennis Buckley, provided the personal information.

7. George Wilder, Harriet Wilder, and Horace Wilder were all the children of Silas Wilder and Sylvia Holmes. George married Elizabeth Darring. They became the parents of Jimmy Wilder, the first Rap-Shaw Club steward. Horace married Cornelia Smith. They became the parents of Elmer Wilder, owner of the famous Camp Happy on Salmon Lake along the Red Horse Chain. Harriet married Joseph Schmidlin. They became the parents of Minnie Schmidlin, who married Harlow Young.

8. This open camp is noted in the reminiscences of J. P. Rapalje, discussed in chapter 12.

9. US Census for 1900 provides Harlow Young's occupation and address.

10. Harlow Young operated this store from 1902 until 1908. The store probably opened in 1902 because Harlow was appointed postmaster that year. He sold the

house in Utica in 1903. *Lewis County Democrat*, Oct. 7,1903. He rented the upstairs to a minister in 1905. *Lowville Journal and Republican*, Feb.23, 1905.

11. List of appointments as US postmaster accessed on Ancestry.com.

12. *Lowville Journal and Republican*, Feb. 15, 1906.

13. They sold the Crystaldale store to Nicholas Ossant in 1908. *Lowville Journal and Republican*, Dec. 16, 1908.

14. Handwritten postcards between Henry Beach and Harlow Young are in the Dennis Buckley collection.

15. Beach is now one of the most recognizable and collectible early Adirondack photographers. Bogdan, *Adirondack Vernacular*.

16. Just before he sold the Old Homestead to Harlow Young, H. C. Churchill built a cottage nearby for his family that they called Forest Home. Forest Home still exists. Prior to the 1925 flooding, it was moved to a waterfront lot in what was to become the settlement of Stillwater. After H. C. and Anna Churchill died, their daughter Alice Churchill Snover inherited the cottage. She sold it to her nephew Jerome Shaver and his wife, Esther. They sold it to their friends Jack and Nancy Fergerson in 1993. The Fergersons sold it to current owners J. R. and Monica Kellogg in 2015.

17. *Lowville Journal and Republican*, Feb. 25, 1915.

18. The Black River Regulating District was formed in 1919 for the specific purpose of building or enlarging dams on the Beaver and Moose Rivers. The details are set forth in chapter 9.

19. *Lowville Journal and Republican*, Apr. 17, 1919.

20. *Lowville Journal and Republican*, Aug. 30, 1923.

21. The new hotel was completed in 1925, and the Young's new camp in 1926.

22. *Watertown Daily Standard*, June 13, 1925.

23. There is some evidence that Harlow Young at one time may have intended to sell the hotel to Loren Singer. Singer may have run the hotel for a short time but his name does not appear in the recorded chain of title. Douglas Purcell and his wife Kate may also have worked for Harlow Young for some years prior to purchasing the hotel.

24. *Black River Democrat*, May 26, 1938.

25. *Lowville Journal and Republican,* June 10, 1938.

26. Minnie died on September 19 and Harlow died on October 5. They are both buried in Beaches Bridge Cemetery outside Lowville on the east bank of the Black River.

27. Information on Emmett and Marge Hill was obtained in a personal interview with retired Forest Ranger Terry Perkins conducted on July 2, 2018. Terry was personally acquainted with the Hills as well as with William Marleau, the ranger at Big Moose Station.

28. Prior to Marleau's time, the Stillwater tower's telephone line ran to Ranger Dave Conkey's cabin at Beaver River Station; Marleau, *Big Moose Station*, 210.

29. On early road improvements see *Lowville Journal and Republican*, Apr. 20, 1922, and Aug. 23, 1923.

30. "New Road in the Wilderness," Dante O. Tranquille, *Utica Observer Dispatch*, Oct. 2, 1955.

31. Thompson, *Beaver River*, 125–29.

32. The information on the Mahoneys was obtained in a personal interview with retired ranger Terry Perkins conducted on July 2, 2018.

## 14. The Stillwater Community

1. This conclusion is based on early maps, including the 1876 map included in Wallace, *Guide*; the 1878 Verplanck Colvin map; the 1880 Seneca Ray Stoddard map; the 1890 New York State Forest Commission map of the Adirondack Park; and the 1895 Joseph Rudolf Bein map of Hamilton, Herkimer Counties.

2. The footings for this bridge still exist underwater as revealed in the 2001 drawdown.

3. Note that the Jim and Clara Dunbar farm was *not* located on Dunbar Island, but rather on what was then the mainland along the road leading to the dam.

4. Clara Dunbar died in 1914. Jim Dunbar married Lucy H. Fenton in the spring of 1915. The couple, both in their fifties, lived at Stillwater, where Jim Dunbar continued to work as the state dam-keeper.

5. This cottage was originally known as the Hayden cottage. It was built on lot 21 of the Beaver River Club for S. E. Hayden from Syracuse. Hayden was one of the original members of the Beaver River Club. He bought lot 21 before 1898. Given its log construction and its location next to the clubhouse, this camp was likely originally built in the mid-1890s.

6. This parcel appears on the 1916 Hopkins map. Tax records for the town of Webb show that Young may have purchased the property on higher ground as early as 1910.

7. Harlow C. Young and Minnie J. Young, his wife, of the town of Lowville, Lewis County, NY, to John Kloster and Florence Kloster, his wife, Frank J. Boshart and E. Lillian Boshart, his wife, Mason L. Webster and Hattie Webster, his wife, Myron M. Lyman and Lydia Lyman, his wife, all of Lowville. This deed was dated Dec. 23, 1919. Nathan Vary, one of the current owners, provided this title information.

8. The original camp building was demolished about thirty years ago to make room for a successor, the current Vary-Roberts camp.

9. As noted at the end of chapter 11, only a few of the Beaver River Club cottages were saved, including those moved to Williams Island and the cottage moved

to the lot purchased by Dancey in Stillwater. A Henry M. Beach photo postcard from about 1925 shows two more cottages, likely from the Beaver River Club, on land owned by Harlow Young in front of the hotel. They were moved to unknown locations shortly thereafter.

10. This information is drawn from the 1912 USGS map of the area and from the 1916 Hopkins map of the Beaver River Club.

11. William Fay Smith was also known as Fay William Smith.

12. It is possible that salvage from the Dunbar farm was used to construct the Fisher Forestry camp at the south end of the hamlet. Albert Dunbar, younger brother of Jim Dunbar, was the superintendent of the Fisher Forestry and Realty Company at the time and could easily have arranged for the salvage. The Fisher Forestry camp burned in 1946.

13. The twelve cottages existing in 1925 were owned by Harlow Young, H. C. Churchill, W. H. Dancey, William Fay Smith, Jacob Zimmerman, the Kloster group, I. S. Foster, Deat Harrington, Clarence Hicks, Carl McCormick, Carl Rowley, and Fisher Forestry. This information is based on the 1925 and 1930 Fisher Forestry & Realty Co. maps of Stillwater hamlet.

14. *Watertown Daily Standard*, June 13, 1925. An identical article appeared in the *Lowville Journal and Republican* on June 25, 1925, and in the *Rome Daily Sentinel* on June 29, 1925. A similar story appeared in the *Utica Daily Press* on July 25, 1925.

15. Siblings Clarence L. Fisher and Florence Fisher Jackson inherited Fisher Forestry & Realty Co. in 1915 after the death of their mother, Mary Lyon Fisher.

16. Hugh R. Jones, *Beaver Lake Country* (New York: Fisher Forestry & Realty Co., 1923), 17 pages, with photographs and maps. Copies are extremely rare but exist in the Adirondack Research Library of the Adirondack Experience Museum at Blue Mountain Lake and at the Beinecke Rare Book Library at Yale University.

17. Caldwell, *This Little Bit of Paradise*, 50.

18. Caldwell, *This Little Bit of Paradise*, 24–29.

19. A map showing all forty-three properties is in Caldwell, *This Little Bit of Paradise*, 46–47. An excellent account of each camp is found on pp. 48–68.

20. The camps built by Wilder are identified in Caldwell, *This Little Bit of Paradise*. Ms. Caldwell was kind enough to arrange for the author to visit the Wilder camps of Carolyn Malkin and Mary Reed Earl on July 3, 2018.

21. *Lowville Journal and Republican*, Jan. 12, 1922. Access to the plot north of the reservoir was maintained by a bridge over the river immediately below the dam. That bridge still exists. For access to the plot east of Twitchell Creek, the state promised that the Black River Regulating District would provide a ferry service from the Stillwater Landing to the remains of the Carthage-to-Lake Champlain Road leading to Beaver River Station. This promise was not kept and Fisher Forestry subsequently sold its property on that side of the reservoir to the state.

22. The APA definition of "hamlet" differs from New York State's general definition of a hamlet as any settled area without its own governing body.

23. See details and map at https://www.apa.ny.gov/Documents/Reports/Hamlets/3-Study-Elements3.pdf.

24. Unless otherwise noted, the information for this section comes from personal interviews with Terry Perkins conducted during July 2018.

25. Donnelly, *History of Beaver River*, 34–35, and interview with Terry Perkins on June 14, 2015.

26. Edith Pilcher, "Paddling Stillwater Reservoir," *Conservationist*, July/Aug. 1981.

27. These roads are kept clear in the winter, but many winter visitors arrive by snowmobile. Once the snow is deep enough or the reservoir freezes solid, it is possible to easily reach Beaver River Station by snow machine.

28. An excellent description of conditions at Beaver River can be found in Mary Feiss, "The Way It Is in Beaver River," *Adirondack Life* (Apr. 1978).

# Bibliography

Amrhein, Cindy. *A History of Native American Land Rights in Upstate New York*. Charleston, SC: History Press, 2016.

Barlow, Jane A., ed. *Big Moose Lake in the Adirondacks*. Syracuse, NY: Syracuse Univ. Press, 2004.

Beach, Nelson. *Journal of Proceedings Relative to the Carthage and Lake Champlain Road*. Transcription by Noel Sherry. Collection of the Lewis County Historical Society.

Bogdan, Robert. *Adirondack Vernacular: The Photography of Henry M. Beach*. Syracuse, NY: Syracuse Univ. Press, 2003.

Bolles, Frank Jr. "A Trip to Albany Lake on Snowshoes." *Forest and Stream* 4 (1875): 197.

Bourcier, Paul G. *History in the Mapping: Four Centuries of Adirondack Cartograph*. Catalog of the exhibit, June 15, 1984–October 15, 1984. Blue Mountain Lake, NY: Adirondack Museum, 1986.

Brown, Henry A. L., and Richard J. Walton. *John Brown's Tract: Lost Adirondack Empire*. Canaan, NH: Published for the Rhode Island Historical Society by Phoenix Pub, 1988.

Brumley, Charles. *Guides of the Adirondacks: A History*. Utica, NY: North Country Books, 1994.

Burnett, Charles Howard. *Conquering the Wilderness: The Building of the Adirondack & St. Lawrence Railroad by William Seward Webb, 1891–92*. Norwood, MA: Privately printed by Mrs. W. Seward Webb, 1932.

Caldwell, Christa. *This Little Bit of Paradise: Beaver Lake at No. 4*. New York: Lewis County Historical Society, 2015.

Cameron, Duncan H. "Adirondack Railways: Historic Engine of Change." *Adirondack Journal of Environmental Studies* 19, no. 1 (2013): Article 4.

Colvin, Verplanck. *Seventh Annual Report on the Progress of the Topographical Survey of the Adirondack Region of New York to the Year 1879*. Albany, NY: Weed, Parsons and Company, 1880.

Curth, Louis C. *The Forest Rangers: A History of the New York State Forest Ranger Force*. Albany, NY: New York State Department of Environmental Conservation, 1987.

DeSormo, Maitland. *The Heydays of the Adirondacks*. Saranac Lake, NY: Adirondack Yesteryears, 1974.

Donaldson, Alfred L. *A History of the Adirondacks*. 2 vols. New York: Century Co., 1921.

Donnelly, William B. *A Short History of Beaver River*. Private publication for the Beaver River Property Owners Association, 1979.

Feiss, Mary. "The Way It Is in Beaver River." *Adirondack Life* (Apr. 1978).

Fisher, Clarence L. "Adirondack Mountains, Number Four Settlement." *Black River Democrat*, Sept. 21, 1922.

Folwell, Elizabeth. "Our Air Force: A Who's Who of North Country Aviators." *Adirondack Life* (Sept./Oct. 2004): 72–79.

Fox, James. *Stillwater Fire Tower: A Centennial History . . . and Earlier*. New York: Friends of Stillwater Fire Tower, 2019.

Gilborn, Craig. *Adirondack Camps: Home Away from Home*. Syracuse, NY: Syracuse Univ. Press, 2000.

Gove, Bill. *Logging Railroads of the Adirondacks*. Syracuse, NY: Syracuse Univ. Press, 2006.

Grady, Joseph F. *The Adirondacks, Fulton Chain–Big Moose Region: The Story of a Wilderness*. 3rd ed. Utica, NY: North Country Books, 1972.

Graham, Frank Jr. *The Adirondack Park, a Political History*. New York: Knopf, 1978.

Ham, John M. and Timothy R. Mayers. *The New York Central in the Adirondacks*. Hunter, NY: Stony Clove & Catskill Mountain Press, 2015.

Harnden, Philip. "Whose Land? An Introduction to Iroquois Land Claims in New York State." American Friends Service Committee, February 2000. https://courses.cit.cornell.edu/govt313/lc/texts/whoseland.pdf.

Harris, Glenn. "The Hidden History of Agriculture in the Adirondack Park, 1825–1875." *New York History* 83, no. 2 (Spring 2002): 165–202.

Harter, Henry A. *Fairy Tale Railroad*. Utica, NY: North Country Books, 1979.

Hartman, Pat. *A Butcher in Beaver River: Edwin Butcher in the Adirondacks*. Privately published, 2017.

Headley, Joel T. *The Adirondack; or, Life in the Woods*. 1849. Reprinted with introduction by Philip G. Terrie. Bovina Center, NY: Harbor Hill Books, 1982.

Heller, Murray. *Call Me Adirondack: Names and Their Stories*. Saranac Lake, NY: Chauncy Press, 1989.

Herr, Charles E. *The Fulton Chain: Early Settlement, Roads, Steamboats, Railroads and Hotels*. Inlet, NY: HerrStory Publications, 2017.

Hill, W. W. "The Beaver River Country, N. Y." *Forest and Stream* 3, no. 1 (Aug. 1874).

———. "The Beaver River Country." *Forest and Stream* 2, no. 24 (July 23, 1874).

Hopper, Raymond G. "Primeval Adirondacks." *Forest and Stream* 36, no. 22 (June 18, 1891): 432–33.

Hough, Franklin B. *History of Lewis County, New York, with Illustrations and Biographical Sketches of Some of Its Prominent Men and Pioneers*. Syracuse, NY: Mason, 1883.

Hyde, F. Russell. "Fishing Trophies." *Rap-Shaw Review* 1, no. 2 (June 1950).

Hyde, F. Russell. "Trophies Awarded! Fishermen, Hide Your Heads." *Rap-Shaw Review* 1, no. 3 (Oct. 1950).

Jacoby, Karl. *Crimes Against Nature: Squatters, Poachers, Thieves and the Hidden History of American Conservation*. Berkley, CA: Univ. of California Press, 2001.

Jamieson, Paul F. *Adirondack Canoe Waters: North Flow*. Glens Falls, NY: Adirondack Mountain Club, 1981.

———. *Adirondack Pilgrimage*. Glens Falls, NY: Adirondack Mountain Club, 1986.

———. "The First White Man Comes to St. Lawrence County." *St Lawrence County Historical Association Quarterly* (Apr. 1968): 3–4, 21–23.

Jones, Hugh R. *Beaver Lake Country*. New York: Fisher Forestry & Realty Co., 1923.

Kaiser, Harvey. *Great Camps of the Adirondacks*. Jaffrey, NH: David R. Godine, 1982.

Kourofsky, Niki. *Adirondack Outlaws: Bad Boys and Lawless Ladies*. Helena, MT: Farcountry Press, 2015.

Kudish, Michael. *Mountain Railroads of New York State, Volume Two: Where Did the Tracks Go in the Central Adirondacks?* Bovina Center, NY: Purple Mountain Press, 2007.

———. *Railroads of the Adirondacks: A History*. Bovina Center, NY: Purple Mountain Press, 1996.

Landis, Norm, and Bradly A. Pendergraft. *Western Trails Book and Map Pack*. Glens Falls, NY: Adirondack Mountain Club, 2016.

Lintner, J. A. "Mr. Otto Meske's Collection of Lepidoptera." *Transactions of the Albany Institute*, vol. 8. Albany, NY: J. Munsell, 1876, 215–20.

Marleau, William. *Big Moose Station*. Van Nuys, CA: Marleau Family Press, 1986.

Martin, Roscoe C. *Water for New York*. Syracuse, NY: Syracuse Univ. Press, 1960.

McEntee, Jervis. "Diary for 1851." Manuscript and typescript, MS 67-019, Adirondack Experience Library, Blue Mountain Lake, NY.

———. "The Lakes of the Wilderness." *Great Republic Monthly*, Apr. 1, 1859, 335–50.

McMartin, Barbara. *The Great Forest of the Adirondacks*. Utica, NY: North Country Books, 1994.

———. *The Privately Owned Adirondacks: Sporting and Family Clubs, Private Parks and Preserves, Timberlands and Easements*. Chicago: Lakeview Press, 2004.

———. *To the Lake of the Skies: The Benedicts in the Adirondacks*. Chicago: Lakeview Press, 1996.

Miller, Seaver Asbury. "The Sporting Clubs in the Adirondacks." *Outing* 32 (1914): 475–82.

Montgomery, Gladys. *An Elegant Wilderness: Great Camps and Grand Lodges of the Adirondacks, 1855–1935*. New York: Acanthus Press, 2011.

Morgan, Lewis H. *The League of the Iroquois*. 1851. Reprint. New York: Citadel Press, 1962.

Morris, William F. "A Trip to the Adirondacks in the Days before Automobiles." *Baldwinsville Gazette and Farmers' Journal*, July 14, 1887.

Murray, William H. H. *Adventures in the Wilderness, or, Camp-life in the Adirondacks*. Boston: Fields, Osgood & Co., 1869.

Nash, Roderick F. *Wilderness and the American Mind*. New Haven, CT: Yale Univ. Press, 1967.

Northrup, A. Judd. *Camps and Tramps in the Adirondacks, and Grayling Fishing in Northern Michigan: A Record of Summer Vacations in the Wilderness*. Syracuse, NY: Davis, Bardeen & Co., 1880.

Otis, Melissa. *Rural Indigenousness: A History of Iroquoian and Algonquian Peoples of the Adirondacks*. Syracuse, NY: Syracuse Univ. Press, 2018.

Pilcher, Edith. *The Constables, First Family of the Adirondacks*. Utica, NY: North Country Books, 1992.

———. "Paddling Stillwater Reservoir." *Conservationist*, July/Aug. 1981, 10–13, 47.

Pitts, Edward I. *The History of the Rap-Shaw Club: 1896 until 1958*. Self-published, 2019.

———. "Butterfly Effect." *Adirondack Life*, May/June 2020.

———. "Historic Firsts: Aerial Fish Stocking of Adirondack Waters." *Adirondack Almanack*, May 31, 2017.

———. "Pop Bullock: Notable Beaver River Guide." *Adirondack Almanack*, Feb. 3, 2018.

———. "'Wild Jess' Elliott: Setting the Record Straight." *Adirondack Almanack*, Apr. 15, 2018.

Potter, Orlando B. III and Donald Brandreth Potter. *Brandreth: A Band of Cousins Preserves the Oldest Adirondack Family Enclave*. Utica, NY: North Country Books, 2011.

Prince, J. Dyneley. "Some Forgotten Indian Place-Names in the Adirondacks." *Journal of American Folk-Lore* (Apr. 1900): 123–28.

Reehil, Roy E., and William J. O'Hern. *Adirondack Adventures: Bob Gillespie and Harvey Dunham on French Louie's Trail*. Cleveland, NY: Forager Press, 2012.

Schaefer, Paul. *Defending the Wilderness: The Adirondack Writings of Paul Schaefer*. Syracuse, NY: Syracuse Univ. Press, 1989.

Schneider, Paul. *The Adirondacks: A History of America's First Wilderness*. New York: Henry Holt and Co., 1997.

Schofield, P. F. "The Forest and Water Storage Policy of the State of New York." *Board of Trade Journal* 40–41 (Jan. 3, 1914): 5–9.

Smith, H. Perry. *Modern Babes in the Wood; or, Summerings in the Wilderness. To Which Is Added a Reliable and Descriptive Guide to the Adirondacks by E. R. Wallace*. Hartford, CT: Columbian Book Co., 1872.

Snow, Dean R., Charles T. Gehring, and William A. Starna, eds. *In Mohawk Country: Early Narratives about a Native People*. Syracuse, NY: Syracuse Univ. Press, 1996.

Snyder, Charles E. "John Brown's Tract. An Address by Charles E. Snyder, of Herkimer, Delivered before the Herkimer County Historical Society, December 8, 1896." In *Papers Read before the Herkimer County Historical Society during the Years 1886, 1897 and 1898*, compiled by Arthur T. Smith, 93–107. Herkimer and Ilion, NY: Citizen Publishing Co., 1899.

Sprague, Ken. "The Beaver River Club." *Adirondack Express*, Nov. 13, 2012.

Stager, Jay Curt. "Hidden Heritage." *Adirondack Life*, Mar./Apr. 2017, 54–66.

State of New York. *Annual Report of the Forest Commission for the Year 1893*. 2 vols. Albany, NY: James B. Lyon, State Printer, 1894.

State of New York. *Annual Report of the Forest Commission for the Year 1894*. Albany, NY: James B. Lyon, 1895.

State of New York. *Annual Report of the Forest Commission of the State of New York for the Year Ending December 31, 1891*. Albany, NY: James B. Lyon, State Printer, 1892.

State of New York. *Annual Report of the State Engineer and Surveyor of the State of New York for the Fiscal Year Ending September 30, 1903*. Albany, NY: Oliver A. Quayle, 1904.

State of New York. *Eighth and Ninth Reports of the Forest, Fish and Game Commission of the State of New York (1902–1903)*. Albany, NY: J. B. Lyon Company, Printers, 1903.

State of New York. *Second Annual Report of the Commissioners of Fisheries, Game and Forests of the State of New York*. New York and Albany: Wynkoop Hallenbeck Crawford Co., 1896.

State of New York. *30th Annual Report on the New York State Museum of Natural History*. Albany, NY: Weed, Parsons and Company, 1879.

Stephens, W. Hudson. *Historical Notes of the Settlement on No. 4, Brown's Tract, in Watson, Lewis County, N.Y. with Notices of the Early Settlers*. Utica, NY: Roberts, 1864.

Stoddard, Dwight J. *Notable Men of Central New York; Syracuse and Vicinity, Utica and Vicinity, Auburn, Oswego, Watertown, Fulton, Rome, Oneida, Little Falls. XIX and XX centuries*. Syracuse, NY: Dwight J. Stoddard, 1903.

Stoddard, Seneca Ray. *The Adirondacks: Illustrated*. Albany, NY: Weed, Parsons & Co., 1880.

Sulavik, Stephen B. *Adirondack: Of Indians and Mountains, 1535–1838*. Bovina Center, NY: Purple Mountain Press and the Adirondack Museum, 2005.

Svenson, Sally E. *Blacks in the Adirondacks: A History*. Syracuse, NY: Syracuse Univ. Press, 2017.

Sylvester, Nathaniel Bartlett. *Historical Sketches of Northern New York and the Adirondack Wilderness, Etc.* 1877. Reprint. Peru, NY: Bloated Toe Publishing, 2014.

Terrie, Philip G. *Contested Terrain: A New History of Nature and People in the Adirondacks*. 2nd ed. Syracuse, NY: Syracuse Univ. Press, 2008.

————. *Wildlife and Wilderness: A History of Adirondack Mammals.* Bovina Center, NY: Purple Mountain Press, 1993.

Thompson, H. H. (Henry Hunn). "On the Wilderness Trail." *Forest and Stream* 7 (Sept. 28, 1876): 114.

Thompson, Pat. *Beaver River: Oasis in the Wilderness.* Beaver River, NY: Beaver River Press, 2000.

Tranquille, Dante O. "New Road in the Wilderness." *Utica Observer Dispatch,* Oct. 2, 1955.

Van Diver, Bradford. *Roadside Geology of New York.* Missoula, MT: Mountain Press Publishing Co., 1985.

Varney, George J. "History of Norridgewock, Maine." *A Gazetteer for the State of Maine.* Boston: B. B. Russell, 1886.

Virtanen, Michael. "Judge Rules for Landowners in Paddling Case." *Adirondack Explorer,* Dec. 21, 2018.

Waite, David. *Entering the North Woods: Beaver River to Lake Lila.* Self-published, 2015.

Walker, Mabel Gregory. "Sir John Johnson, Loyalist." *Mississippi Valley Historical Review* 3, no. 3 (Dec. 1916).

Wallace, Edwin R. *Descriptive Guide to the Adirondacks: And Handbook of Travel to Saratoga Springs, Schroon Lake, Lakes Luzerne, George, and Champlain, the Ausable Chasm, the Thousand Islands, Massena Springs and Trenton Falls.* Syracuse, NY, multiple editions, 1872–97.

Wessels, William L. *Adirondack Profiles.* Lake George, NY: Adirondack Resorts Press Inc., 1961.

Whitaker, E. S. "Adirondack Tours." *Forest and Stream* 57 (Dec. 7, 1901): 452.

Whitford, Noble E. *History of the Canal System of the State of New York together with Brief Histories of the Canals of the United States and Canada.* New York: New York State Legislative Printer, 1906.

Williams, Michael. *Americans and Their Forests: A Historical Geography.* Cambridge: Cambridge Univ. Press, 1992.

Withington, L. A. "Deer Hunt in the Adirondacks." *Ogdensburg Daily Journal,* Dec. 4, 1903.

Woods, Lynn. "History in Fragments." *Adirondack Life,* Dec. 1994.

Note: This list does not include census materials, citations to the *Laws of the State of New York*, short newspaper articles, maps, or personal interviews.

# Index

*Page numbers appearing in italics refer to illustrations.*

**Edward I. Pitts** is a retired attorney and administrative law judge who lives in Syracuse, New York. He has had a life-long interest in local history, especially of the Adirondacks and Central New York. His articles on Adirondack history have appeared in *Adirondack Life*, *Adirondac* magazine, and *LOCALadk*, and on the *Adirondack Almanack*. He is a regular contributor to the Facebook group History and Legends of the Adirondacks. He is a member of the Rap-Shaw Club on Stillwater Reservoir, where he was president of the board of directors from 2011 until 2016. He has been the club historian from 2016 to the present. His book detailing the history of the Rap-Shaw Club was published in 2019. Before becoming a lawyer, he taught philosophy at St. Bonaventure University and at Pennsylvania State University.

9 780815 611332